William Randolph
HEARST

An Illustrated Biography

by

NANCY E. LOE

Produced by Companion Press
Bishop, California
Jane Freeburg, Publisher/Editor
Printed in Hong Kong

Available exclusively at
Aramark's Hearst Castle® Gift Shop
www.hearstcastleretail.com

ISBN 0-944197-77-9

ACKNOWLEDGMENTS

Many thanks to the following people for their help on this revised and updated edition: Catherine Trujillo of Special Collections, Kennedy Library, California Polytechnic State University, San Luis Obispo; Kate Bentham of the Adams Museum & House, Deadwood, South Dakota; and Stacey Behlmer of the Margaret Herrick Library at the Academy of Motion Pictures Arts and Sciences, Beverly Hills. Special thanks to Ken Kenyon of Special Collections, Kennedy Library, California Polytechnic State University, San Luis Obispo for invaluable assistance on citations and management of photographs; to Jane Freeburg of Companion Press for living proof you can do good work and have fun at the same time; and to George Libby, for keeping the home fires burning.

Nancy Loe
San Luis Obispo, California
March, 2005

ILLUSTRATIONS

Illustrations in this edition are reproduced courtesy of: Adams Museum & House, Deadwood, SD: 19, 25. The Bancroft Library, University of California, Berkeley: 6, 11, 15, 17, 16, 21, 22, 31, 48, 78 upper left, 96, back cover. Bison Archives: 70, 85, 86, 87. British Film Institute: 59. Brown Brothers: 2, 5, 46, 57. California Polytechnic State University, Special Collections Department, Kennedy Library: 9, 17, 20, 27, 33, 34, 36, 60, 64 both, 76, 78 center left, 79 all, 80 bottom, 81 both, 84, 90 bottom; Healy Collection of California Newspapers: 28, 30, 53 bottom; Hearst Caricatures Collection: 42, 47 both, 53 top, 55 top, 56; Cora Older Collection on George Hearst: 3, 52; Julia Morgan Collections: 20, 34, 68 both, 69 both, 72, 73 both, 74, 75, 78 top. ©Hearst Castle®/CA State Parks: Front cover, front flap, 13, 50, 51, 54, 66, 71, 88, 91, back flap. Photofest: 82 both, 83, 89, 90 top. South Dakota State Historical Society–State Archives:18. Private Collections: 1, 12, 39, 41, 44, 55 bottom, 58, 62, 63, 80 top. *Time* ©Time Warner Inc. Used by permission. All rights reserved. *Telegram-Tribune* front page © The Tribune News, Knight Ridder, Inc. All rights reserved.

Contents

CHAPTER ONE

The Early Years

William Randolph Hearst's ground-breaking career began in 1887 with a "miserable little sheet,"[1] a San Francisco newspaper his father owned called the *Examiner*. Spurning his father's offer of a job overseeing the family's vast ranching and mining interests, William Randolph Hearst wrote, "I am possessed of the weakness which at some time or other of their lives pervades most men; I am convinced that I could run a newspaper successfully."[2] From that single paper, Hearst built a media powerhouse, branching from newspapers into magazines, film, radio, and motion pictures.

An endlessly fascinating figure, W.R. Hearst is the subject of nine full-length biographies and numerous articles, oral histories, and reminiscences. Schol-arly theses and dissertations have dissected his influence on American politics and journalism. Others closely study his vast art and architecture holdings. Novelists and filmmakers—most notably Aldous Huxley and Orson Welles—have found Hearst's activities in politics, movie-making, and the media to be rich material for thinly disguised accounts of his life and career.

Although Hearst liked to think of himself as a self-made man, the family fortune started when W.R.'s father George struck it rich on the Comstock Lode, beginning the trans-formation of the Hearst family from nameless pioneers to a dynasty that influences American life to this day.

The founder of the Hearst family in America was John Hurst, a Scottish

Young Willie Hearst spent his early years in San Francisco.

Presbyterian who arrived in Virginia in 1680, and settled in Isle of Wight County. The Old English spelling of the name was "Hyrst," meaning a group of trees or a thicket. After two generations in America, the family resided in Bertie County, North Carolina, where the English spelling of Hurst was changed to Hearst. John Hearst III married Elizabeth Knox and moved to Abbeville County, South Carolina, in 1776. John and Elizabeth Knox Hearst's third son, George, left South Carolina in 1808 for a homestead in the recently acquired Louisiana Purchase. Land along the Merrimack River, not far from present-day Sullivan, Missouri, attracted the first George Hearst, for it suited the twin interests of the family: livestock production and mining. George Hearst, his wife, and their two sons, William G. and Joseph, prospered at the new homestead.

William G. Hearst married Elizabeth Collins in 1817. They moved farther west on government land in what is now southwest Texas. Troubled by sickness and financial reverses, they returned to their families in Missouri after two years. On September 3, 1820, their first child, George Hearst, was born on the family's Missouri farm and named for his South Carolina pioneering grandfather. At the time George Hearst was born, his family was the most prosperous in Meramec Township, owning at least 120 acres of land and nineteen slaves.

Although George worked throughout his youth on the family farm, his true interest lay in mining, sparked by the prospectors his father had hired to work claims on the family land.

After limited local schooling, George Hearst enrolled at the Franklin County Mining School in 1838. He was remembered by neighbors as

> a raw country youth of 19 [who] tramped the hills and hollows barefooted, pantaloons rolled up to the knees, amusing himself by chasing hogs from their midday baths, cool[ing] his blistered feet in the muddy depths of the hog wallow.[3]

In November of 1844, William G. Hearst died, leaving a widow, Elizabeth; a daughter, Martha; and two sons, George and Jacob. Hearst's will described Jacob as "rendered helpless by disease" and made provisions for his care and support. In less than two years Jacob also was dead. In 1848 Elizabeth Collins Hearst remarried, taking as her husband a postmaster and former county judge, Joseph Funk.

A year later, news of the fabulous gold strikes in California reached Missouri, and George was no longer content managing the family land and other business holdings. He said his farewells to his family and headed west. Six women and eight other men, including his cousins, Joseph and James Clark, comprised the overland group. George contracted a severe case of cholera after about a month on the California trail, separating him from his cousins and the rest of the original Missouri party, who were forced to continue without him. Once Hearst recovered sufficiently to be able to mount his horse and ride, he was able to rejoin the Missourians after several days of hard travel. Not far from Fort Laramie, Hearst and his friends and relatives celebrated their reunion with a dinner of dried buffalo meat, potatoes, hot biscuits, and wild honey.

On the Fourth of July, an important holiday for emigrants who had left the United States behind when they headed west, George Hearst and his fellow travelers arrived in Fort Laramie. Not daring to sacrifice a whole day to the holiday celebration, they enjoyed an extended noonday meal that was topped off with St. Louis brandy, the firing of guns and a spirited rendition of the National Anthem. They then resumed their journey, spurred by talk of bad weather and stories of the Donner Party tragedy four winters before, as well as conflicting reports that the gold country was booming or had almost tapped out.

Nearly six months out of Missouri, and in average time despite their adversities, they arrived at the South Fork of the American River in northern California. Hearst and his companions headed first for Diamond Springs, then to Hangtown and finally on to Jackass Gulch, where recent promising strikes

George Hearst (1820–1891)

had been made. Their entire winter's work resulted in only a meager standard of gold camp living. Cora Older, George Hearst's biographer, reports that his mining career was "no tale of easy, sudden success. So little was his gain that sometimes he said Jackass Gulch was well-named." Hearst and his cousins abandoned their claim in the spring of 1851 when he "knew that he and the Clarks would never be millionaires by washing gold in that unyielding granite canyon. The dust simply wasn't there."[4]

For the next seven years George continued to stake claims throughout the northern California gold fields. Early in 1858, George's stepfather, Joseph Funk, sent news of George's Missouri properties and asked him to return home to visit his aging mother. Hearst responded in March by sending $300 to his mother, writing, "My chances are pretty good to make money at present… If the claim…holds out as it has so far, it is one of the good things that is sometimes found in California." As for his return, he wrote to his stepfather,

> I would like to see you and mother…much better than you suppose, but to come home without money is out of the question; but if I have any kind of luck I will come

home soon and stop awhile, though I do not expect to make [Missouri] my home; I am satisfied I could not stand that climate."[5]

As George continued to hunt for a fortune from the earth, life on the trail became natural to him. He prospected on the western slope of the Sierra until July of 1859, when the Comstock Lode was discovered near the present-day town of Carson City, Nevada. George Hearst and his compatriots traveled east over the Sierra on pack mules, part of the "great backward rush from California." Although eager gold miners had prospected the Comstock mining area for the past ten years with some success, Hearst later recalled "heavy black stuff" that clogged the mining pans and rockers of those who only thought of gold. George quietly tested for silver content and then quickly staked a claim, named it the Ophir and set about proving his hunch.

In March of 1860, almost ten years after leaving Missouri, George Hearst realized $80,000 from his mine. He bought another claim, the Gould & Curry, to add to his original Ophir holdings. A new mining camp, Virginia City, sprang up as Comstock claims paid handsomely.

Hearst invested a portion of his new fortune in other mines, banked another portion and then decided to make his long-awaited trip back to Missouri and his mother, so he could "see her have all that life could desire."[6]

Once home, George found his mother "very low with consumption" and his Missouri land holdings in jeopardy because of his long absence and the unexpected death of his business associate, William Patton. He spent seven months with his mother at her home, until Elizabeth Hearst Funk died on April 1, 1861. Untangling his business problems occupied George in Missouri for another eighteen months.

Now 40 years old, George also began to search for a wife. He reacquainted himself with his neighbors, including Phoebe Elizabeth Apperson, the eighteen-year-old daughter of Randolph Walker and Drucilla Whitmire Apperson. The Appersons were also a prosperous, slave-owning family with Virginia and South Carolina antecedents. Their daughter, nicknamed "Puss," was born on the family farm in Franklin County, Missouri, on December 3, 1842. (Throughout her early life and well into adulthood, she spelled her name Phebe, but late in life and for unexplained reasons, she altered her name to the more traditional spelling.)

According to George Hearst's biographer,

> Phebe Elizabeth Apperson was mystical, different from the women he had seen in the past ten years; determined, rugged women of the prairie schooners; women of the fandango houses; women who could us a rocker like a man. Phebe Elizabeth Apperson was a vision. She had

grace and charm and touches of humor like his own. Though she had been brought up in a log cabin she could play the piano. She stammered French. She was eager to learn."[7]

Phoebe had attended the rural county school and received further schooling under a St. Louis governess, but she longed for a wider education. Because George Hearst had received, at most, two years of formal education, family or friends did not take his courtship of the intellectual Phoebe seriously. When he continued to call upon her, Phoebe's parents objected to any match between them, primarily because of the difference in their ages.

Although Hearst's biographer writes that George was "too modest" to tell Phoebe of his Nevada silver mine, news of his prosperity had preceded him. The day before they eloped on June 15, 1862, to Steelville, Missouri, George Hearst and Phoebe Apperson entered into a prenuptial legal agreement. She agreed to marry George, who in turn conveyed fifty shares of Gould and Curry mining stock to Phoebe for "her exclusive use as long as she lived."[8]

That fall, the newlyweds headed first to St. Louis and then on to New York City, where they boarded a steamer bound for the Isthmus of Panama and, ultimately, San Francisco. On shipboard, the Hearsts made the acquaintance of David and Margaret Peck and their two children, Orrin and

Helen, who were also moving to San Francisco. Seasickness and the early months of pregnancy gave Phoebe Hearst a most difficult passage, which Margaret Peck did her best to alleviate.

In December, the steamer sailed through the Golden Gate, delivering George and Phoebe Hearst to their new home. In 1862, San Francisco had a population of nearly eighty thousand, including

> velvet-footed Chinese with long queues, wearing bright mandarin coats, Indians in blankets, Mexicans in sombreros, American dandies in silk hats and broadcloth, bearded miners, soft-voiced southern women and high-nosed executive New England women.[9]

To Phoebe, who had always longed for broader horizons, the sights and sounds of this bustling city were intoxicating. George and Phoebe Hearst

Phoebe Elizabeth Apperson married George Hearst June 15, 1862.

Phoebe Apperson Hearst with her only child, William Randolph.

first lived at the Lick House, the finest hotel in the city, but shortly moved to the more economical Stevenson House, which stood on the northwest corner of California and Montgomery Streets. Here Phoebe gave birth to her only child, William Randolph Hearst, on April 29, 1863.

Although Phoebe wanted to live with her husband in the mining camps, George thought San Francisco the only respectable place for his wife and son. He decided to make trips back and forth between his family and the Comstock mines two hundred miles away. A brick house on Rincon Hill became the Hearsts' new home.

As George became increasingly involved in his mining ventures, Phoebe turned her time, attention, and intellect to nurturing her son. Although she hoped for the addition of a daughter, Willie remained her only child, to be "mothered, loved, pampered, praised, protected, instructed, fussed over, waited on and worried about every moment of his infant existence."[10] However divergent their interests, the Hearsts shared a great deal of affection and regard for their son, who charmed friends and family alike.

By many accounts, including his own, young William Randolph Hearst was an indulged child. According to one Hearst biographer, W.A. Swanberg, "Willie was given just about everything he wanted, including a pony and a cart and a Punch and Judy show in the

barn." His mother called him Willie; his father nicknamed him "Billy Buster." He was given two dogs, beginning a lifetime of affectionate regard for dogs and other animals he attempted to domesticate as pets.

An Irish wet nurse, Eliza Pike, joined the family for three years, becoming as devoted to infant Willie as his mother. Phoebe then prevailed upon her parents and brother to abandon Missouri for a ranch in Santa Clara County. As a youngster, Willie would spend a great deal of time at the Apperson ranch when his mother was traveling and his father was pursuing yet another remote mining claim.

Phoebe also turned her formidable energy to the task of winning a place in mid-nineteenth century San Francisco high society, whose social standards were based first on wealth and then on background and breeding. By these measures, the Hearsts excelled, for George Hearst sought wealth as assiduously as Phoebe courted culture. Their child would inherit their determination for and love of both worlds in almost equal measure.

Known as an elegant hostess, Phoebe also craved recognition as a cultural leader. The family left Rincon Hill for a larger house on the southwest corner of Chestnut and Leavenworth Streets, where Phoebe began to satisfy her lifelong desire for learning and self-improvement. She hosted literary society meetings, *musicales* and other *divertissements* featuring writers, painters, sculptors, and musicians. To prepare herself for the task of guiding young Willie's future education, Phoebe took private language lessons, visited art museums and galleries, and attended the opera.

Her husband, who loathed such activities, did not accompany her on her cultural excursions. A society reporter wrote of seeing George come home early one afternoon, only to find a *musicale* in progress. He skirted the parlor "in his stocking feet, carefully carrying his boots in his right hand… He looked neither to right nor to left, but glided through the apartment like a ghost, to the intense amusement of the guests."[11]

George Hearst spent his days attending to his mining interests and mixing in Democratic politics. In 1865, George won a seat in the State Assembly, but decided against running for reelection. He also began purchasing lots in downtown San Francisco, and paid $30,000 for 40,000 acres of ranchland along the central coast of California, including the original Mexican ranchos of San Siméon, Piedras Blancas, and Santa Rosa.

George Hearst's reputation as a shrewd judge of mining claims was now well established. Prospectors, investors, and speculators followed Hearst's travels, alert to potential leads to new digs and rich claims. In the summer of 1872, George Hearst arrived at a

mining camp called Park City, thirty-five miles southeast of Salt Lake City. There he met with two Canadian miners who were discouraged by the hard work they had invested in their claims with little tangible reward. On behalf of himself and his partner, James Ben Ali Haggin,[12] George Hearst offered them $27,000 for the Ontario mine, as well as $3,000 to another man who claimed an interest. For the first three years the account books were kept in red ink. Sizable amounts of capital were necessary to build rock crushers, mills, and smelters in the mountains near Parley's Peak. These expenditures greatly strained Hearst's financial resources, leading the Hearst family to retrench and sell off assets. By the end of 1876, the firm of Hearst & Haggin had netted $1.1 million from their Park City interests. From 1877 to George Hearst's death in 1891, the Ontario

The Piedras Blancas lighthouse is situated on the coast near the village of San Simeon, where George Hearst began acquiring large parcels of coastal ranchland in the 1860s.

would yield more than $12 million, providing bedrock for the Hearst fortune and George's continuing speculation in mines, ranchland, and commercial real estate.

Phoebe's growing interest in the arts could no longer be sated by trips to local galleries and literary gatherings of her friends. Only an eighteen-month Grand Tour of Europe, that status symbol of the rising Gilded Age, could satisfy Phoebe. After consulting Baedeker's guidebooks and retaining the services of a private tutor for her son, Phoebe left San Francisco with Willie in the early spring of 1873, just before he turned ten. They traveled East on the four-year-old transcontinental railroad, a remarkable advance in comfort and speed over George's hazardous overland journey little more than twenty years earlier.

Phoebe, with typical determination, decided to write to George in the form of a diary so complete that he would be able to share their experiences. Her account begins on March 25, 1873, in Sullivan, Missouri, where they had stopped to visit friends and relatives. "Willie was not well yesterday had sore throat," Phoebe wrote, "but feels bright today he is so delighted with the snow. I shall be very careful of him, as you well know he is quite the little escort for me…."[13]

They sailed for Great Britain on the *Adriatic* in April. The Hearst party's itinerary included Ireland, Scotland, England, Germany, Switzerland, France, and Italy. Swanberg writes,

> For the average boy of ten, a year and a half in Europe would be a dreary eternity…[but] Willie Hearst was no average boy. He showed a keen interest in what he saw that saved him from boredom and showed a maturing intellect. He had a lively sense of pity. In Dublin he was troubled by the sight of overworked horses and by a depth of poverty he had never seen in America.[14]

One of George's real estate partners, William Lent, was also sending his wife and ten-year-old son abroad that year. The Lents and the Hearsts crossed paths on a number of occasions, providing Willie with the company of Eugene, who was definitely an "average boy of ten," more interested in antics than art.

During this formative journey, two passions were awakened in young Willie Hearst that would shape his adult life: traveling abroad and collecting art. The lessons that Phoebe planned with her son's private tutor coincided beautifully with their travels. Willie was able to read about medieval Britain as they toured the lost keeps of England, Scotland, Wales, and Ireland.

Phoebe wrote that "Willie would have liked to live" at Windsor Castle.[15] The German language and its folklore were studied as they sailed down the Rhine, stopping for tours of the schlosses that lined the banks. Verona,

Florence, Rome, and Venice provided powerful artistic images from the Renaissance that Hearst would one day rely upon when planning his estate at San Simeon.

Nine months into their journey, Willie appears to have exhausted even the redoubtable Phoebe, who confided in a letter to her husband she believed Willie "is getting a mania for travel…"[16] From Antwerp, Phoebe wrote,

> This afternoon will visit the Tomb of Rubens…and then go to a fair, where Willie is anxious to go. I do not feel equal to it, but he gets lonely and I must indulge him in some things.[17]

Willie's lifelong zest for collecting began with German beer steins. By the time they reached Switzerland, Phoebe records that Willie "wants all of the carvings in wood that we see. They are very tempting, so many beautiful things… [so] I will get him a few little articles."[18] In mid-November they moved on to Italy, about which Willie was particularly enthusiastic. During their lengthy stay in Florence, Phoebe "had difficulty convincing Willie there were other places to see & that we could not buy all we saw. He gets so fascinated his reason and judgment forsake him. I too acknowledge the temptation…."[19]

The artistic sights prompted Willie to ask his mother for drawing lessons. She anxiously consulted George by mail:

> He is picture crazy. I do not mean to say he has any special talent and would not wish him an artist (unless a great one) but he frequently surprises me in his expressions concerning the best pictures. If he only learns to sketch enough to amuse & interest himself I should be glad.[20]

When his wife and son left California, George Hearst was in a precarious financial position. The Ontario had yet to turn a profit and still required great infusions of capital. A short time later, the national Bank Panic of 1873 and resulting economic depression wrought havoc with the price of gold and silver, further complicating George's business affairs.

Perhaps sensing that their discretionary funds were running low, Phoebe suggested in one letter that they cut short their trip and reduce their expenses. "Willie must go into [public] school & I shall follow you. I have no hope of having you settle down at home & now I should be *terribly* lonely, when you are away."[21] Despite the state of the family finances, the moment passed and Phoebe and her son instead completed their extended tour of Europe, arriving in New York City on October 23, 1874.

However, upon their return to San Francisco, strict economy was practiced until the future of the Ontario mine in Park City was no longer in doubt. They sold the Chestnut Street home, their horses and carriages, dismissed the servants and, most startling of all,

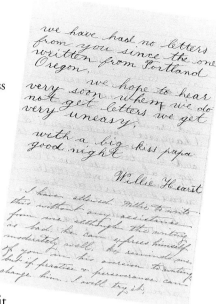

As an addendum to one of ten-year-old Willie's letters to his father, Phoebe wrote: "I have allowed Willie to write this without any assistance from me. Although the writing is bad, he can express himself moderately well. He reminds me of you in his aversion to writing, but if practice and perseverance can change him, I will try it."

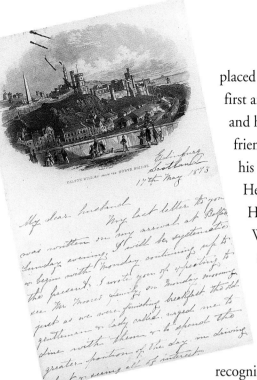

On May 17, 1873, Phoebe wrote to her husband of her travels through Scotland with young Willie.

placed Willie in public school for the first and only time in his life. He and his mother boarded with friends, while his father resumed his business travels. For George Hearst, there was no sacrifice. He was happiest roaming the West on horseback, bartering $20 gold pieces for tidbits of information about new strikes.

The Black Hills— sacred to the Sioux—were recognized by the United States as part of the Great Sioux Reservation in the Treaty of 1868. Six years later, gold was discovered in the course of an expedition led by Lt. Col. George Armstrong Custer's Seventh Cavalry. Treaties meant nothing to the prospectors, investors, tenderfeet, merchants, and opportunists, who streamed onto Sioux land and set up a lawless camp called Deadwood, outside the reach of U. S. law. Enraged by the desecration of their sacred sites, the Sioux and their allies overwhelmed and killed Custer and his troops at the Little Bighorn River on June 25, 1876, further inflaming popular sentiment to break the government's 1868 treaty.

George Hearst first learned of the Black Hills strikes in August of 1875 from "a wild fellow that when broke always used to come to me to get money." But Hearst was so overextended financially because of the Ontario mine that he was unable to

act immediately on this latest tip. A year later, when the Ontario at last began to yield a flood of high-grade silver ore, George Hearst immediately dispatched the Ontario's superintendent to the Black Hills, "but the Indians got so bad that it was as much as a man's life was worth to go there," and the trip was aborted. In the early months of 1877, a Hearst agent named John Sevenoaks made it to Deadwood and sent his boss a flurry of telegrams so compelling that Hearst rushed in reinforcements and started raising capital in San Francisco. He directed his agents to pay $70,000 to brothers Fred and Moses Manuel, who had made a lucky strike in April of 1876. They named their claim the "Homestake" because they hoped it would provide their stake to return home.[22]

By summer, Hearst himself had arrived in Lead, the boomtown closest to his Black Hills claims. A survey of the Homestake and neighboring claims convinced him that its promise was almost beyond imagination. "While the quartz is not very rich," Hearst wrote to Haggin, "the amount of quartz that will pay a profit is truly enormous. You nor your children will live to see the time when this mine will not be worked for a profit."[23] Hearst and Haggin added another partner to their syndicate, Lloyd Tevis, president of Wells Fargo. Tevis was also Haggin's brother-in-law and served as George's principal lawyer for business affairs.[24]

"Anyone who had seen the cycle as often as Hearst could tell that Lead City was taking off," one historian wrote, "riding the curve of a boom that promised to be big. To Hearst it was *déja vu*, Virginia City all over again. With Ontario money behind him now, he didn't mean to get in on the boom. He meant to take it over."[25]

George Hearst succeeded. He pursued 250 separate claims on 2,616 acres, combining them into one gigantic mining claim, which he still called the Homestake. By August of 1879 the Hearst syndicate owned every major mine on the Deadwood Lode, except one, which was eventually secured in 1881. Some were bought out by hypnotically high prices; others, lacking the Hearst syndicate's capital resources, were forced to sell; still others fought in court and lost against Hearst's battery of lawyers. "As to the lawyers," Hearst noted in a letter to his partner Haggin,

> I think we have made no mistake in retaining Thomas for the reason he is the son-in-law of [the] presiding justice of the Territorial Supreme Court…. We also retain [W.H.] Claggett, for although he may not be a profound lawyer, he has a good insight into mining law and makes a very pretty speech before a jury or court.[26]

George Hearst's unfettered determination to control the Deadwood fields parallels similar methods used by his contemporaries who also acquired vast

wealth. Such single-minded tactics earned the label of robber baron for John D. Rockefeller in the oil fields of Pennsylvania, Andrew Carnegie in Pittsburgh steel production, Jay Gould and Cornelius Vanderbilt in Eastern railroads, and J.P. Morgan in banking.

To his partner James Haggin, Hearst wrote,

> I will hurt a good many people. And it is quite possible that I may get killed, but if I should I can't but lose a few years [he was then 57], and all I ask of you is to see that my wife and child gets all that is due them from all the sources and that I am not buried in this place.[27]

Hearst and his partners invested $10 million in their new claim. The Homestake yielded at least $80 million in its first 20 years of operation, with another $635 million extracted by 1962. The Homestake, which became the largest gold mine in the Western Hemisphere, produced more than 39 million ounces between 1887 and 1997.[28]

The capital and resources at the command of George Hearst and his partners ushered in the era of large-scale mining in the Black Hills. Hearst, Tevis and Haggin invested in milling and refining equipment and bought out neighboring mines that could not

Mining magnate George Hearst purchased one of the most promising gold claims in Deadwood for $70,000 and incorporated it and others as the Homestake Mining Company. It became the oldest, largest, and deepest mine in the Western Hemisphere, reaching more than 8,000 feet below the town of Lead and yielding millions of ounces of gold.

George Hearst's Homestake Mine in the Black Hills of South Dakota, famed as the largest gold mine in the world, brought millions of dollars to the Hearst family fortune.

afford to process deep or low-grade ore. As one historian notes, "Together, they made investing in western mines as close to an exact science as it would ever become."[29]

Hearst and his partners were also early practitioners of the business art of "vertical integration"—buying and/or controlling all the different aspects of making, selling, and delivering a product or service. Hearst's group not only controlled the mines, but also owned water rights yielding $100,000 a year, and the railroad, which supplied timber for the mines and exported ore, netting another $180,000 per year. Hearst reinvested these profits not just in more ore stamping mills and lumber mills, but also into the housing and stores in the company town of Lead, where the mine's employees and their families lived and shopped.

Phoebe and young Willie had gladly resumed the good life when the Ontario began to pay, rehiring domestic help and private tutors, purchasing new

teams and carriages, and buying an outsized house at 734 Sutter Street, a fashionable San Francisco address. The Homestake made possible a move in 1878 to 726 California Street, where the family remained for the next four years. Thirteen-year-old Willie wrote to George:

> It seems a long time since you left us, and we miss you very much. As you have already reached the mines we hope you are more comfortable. Mama said last night she wished you were at home again. I wish so too. I wish I could spend a few days in the Black Hills. I would like to have a shot at some of those deer, elk and maybe grizzly bears I heard you talk about. Bunny took some champagne last night and it made him tight. Mama was very much provoked with me but mad as she was she could not help laughing at him. He has learned to open his cage and now we can scarcely keep it fastened.[30]

In a postscript, Phoebe adds,

> I hope you will avoid "Black Hills" and all Indian countries where there may be danger. We don't want anything to happen to you. The money would be of little value if you could not enjoy it with us.[31]

The success of the Ontario and the promise of the Homestake meant that Phoebe could take a second trip to Europe, which she had once feared she would never have. Will (as he now preferred to be called) would naturally accompany her, and Thomas Barry was enlisted as the private tutor who provided lessons that complemented the surroundings. Eugene Lent and his mother were also making another trip to Europe; plans were made to meet them at a number of stops, including Paris. The early months of 1879 found them all embarking on an uneventful passage to Europe.

Barry kept a diary of the trip, lasting from May to August of 1879, revealing himself as an intensely serious young man, who felt his obligations to educate the mischievous Hearst heir quite keenly.

> FRIDAY, JUNE 6 …After Will's exercise we went to the Louvre and I showed Will the beautiful things in the statuary department—feasting myself again on Venus. Will prefers Vatican Venus… After dinner I took a ride with Mrs. H. and then gave Will his usual lesson and then after reading some and writing some letters for Mrs. H. to her shipping agent in Liverpool and to bankers in London I went to bed after 11…

> SATURDAY, JUNE 7 …Started for Louvre after making Will study a half hour for morning transgressions….

> WEDNESDAY, JUNE 11 …After Will's exercise—during which [he was] rude to [the riding] Master with idiotic attempts at fun which highly amused Eugene—we then went to Pantheon. …After dinner I went out riding with Mrs. H., Will and Eugene to the Bois, which was very lovely. After returning at about 9 we celebrated the occasion with Champagne.

After nearly four months of travel and sightseeing, Phoebe Hearst decided to return to Germany at the close of the summer for an extended stay at a health spa, while Will sailed to America to enroll at St. Paul's, an Eastern prep school, accompanied by Thomas Barry and his friend, Eugene Lent. Barry felt a great need to impart discipline and knowledge to young Will Hearst, a sense of obligation doubled with the absence of Mrs. Hearst.

> At half past ten services were held in the large saloon. Will and I attended. This morning he felt the spiritual influences of the day so strongly that he buttoned his coat up to his throat, donned my broad-brimmed straw hat, placed his spectacles solemnly upon his nose, dragged a seedy pair of gloves upon his hands, carefully tearing down the finger ends, stuck his Latin Dictionary under his arm and walked about the saloon in a slow and solemn fashion to the huge delight of Eugene.[32]

While Phoebe Hearst educated their son in Europe, George Hearst was more at home in the rough mining camp of Deadwood, seen here in 1877.

Phoebe Hearst used this color lithography of her country estate outside San Francisco, the Hacienda del Pozo de Verona, as a Christmas card.

Young Will then traveled to New Hampshire to enroll at St. Paul's, an elite prep school. Hearst was not only homesick for his mother, he also hated the school's regimen and the frigid, bleak New England winters that were a sharp contrast to the pleasant California climate. He flooded Phoebe with a stream of pitiful letters that he hoped would win his freedom:

> …I am working very hard "nine hours per day"and even then can hardly keep up with the form…. I feel very despondent and lonely all the time and wish for you to come awful bad.
>
> It has been over a week since I received a letter, and I feel very anxious for fear you are sick. If you are I would much rather know. It is the next thing to speaking with you to write and receive a letter.
>
> It is all I can do to keep from crying sometimes when [I realize] how much alone I am and how far away you are. …the only thing that comforts me is that the time is getting shorter every day till you will be here….[33]

His letters were effective, for after little more than a year at the New Hampshire school, Phoebe relented and Will returned to San Francisco and resumed his studies with private tutors.

George Hearst continued to travel throughout the West on mining business. In 1881, his agents reported on a silver mine on Anaconda Hill, near Butte, Montana. He telegraphed instructions to buy a quarter-interest in this mine sight unseen, even though it was commonly believed most of the silver and gold in this area had already been discovered during earlier strikes. Hearst left for Montana, carrying, as his son would later recall, suitcases full of ore samples and quartz.

The first assays from the Anaconda were promising for their copper content. Hearst ordered the construction of a smelter, purchased the water rights, and bought the local railroad. From 1881, until George Hearst's death ten years later, over 400 million pounds of copper were taken from the Anaconda. Secure after the Homestake gold strikes, the Hearst family fortune was made invincible by the Anaconda lode. George Hearst continued to roam the West, investigating mines and reinvesting his profits in real estate throughout the West.

Occasionally he and his son would travel 200 miles south to San Simeon ranch to camp and to investigate the progress of the cattle ranching on the property. In 1878, George directed the construction of a pier on San Simeon Bay and a two-story house a short distance from the sea, making it possible for Phoebe to sail down the coast to visit the ranch for the first time since the initial purchase thirteen years earlier.

In 1882 the Hearst family moved

into a suite at the Baldwin, at the northeast corner of Powell and Market. Within a year they had moved to 1501 Van Ness; by 1885 their newest home was on Nob Hill at 1105 Taylor Street. They remained in this address for only a short time, for their various interests led them to spend the balance of the year in the East. After 1886, the Hearsts' primary California residence was the Hacienda del Pozo de Verona estate near Pleasanton.

George's political ambitions were growing apace with his wealth. He made substantial contributions to the Democratic Party and loans in excess of $100,000 to its floundering San Francisco newspaper, the *Examiner*. George became the newspaper's owner in October of 1880 in lieu of repayment of the loans. Although George was unenthusiastic about his newest acquisition, he did concede the importance of maintaining a newspaper that favored his party's interests. However, the newspaper made no difference in his unsuccessful bid for the Democratic nomination for governor of California in 1882. Will first visited the *Examiner*'s offices during the period before he left for college, but no record remains of his initial impressions of journalism.

In the fall of 1882 Will, traveled to Cambridge with his mother and matriculated at Harvard, then open only to male students. At nineteen, Hearst was tall, slender and good-

A portrait of Phoebe Apperson Hearst in the 1890s by F. B. Johnstone.

looking. His voice had not dropped to the lower registers that people expected from a young man of his build. He wore his hair parted precisely in the middle and slicked down with tonic, a style favored by nearly all of his fashionable peers. Given the clannish nature of his Eastern classmates, Will's circle of friends was drawn primarily from the "Cal boys," sons of his father's business partners. Eugene Lent, the childhood companion of his European trips, and Jack Follansbee, an Oakland boy, were his closest friends. He followed college sports avidly and four university clubs counted on his congenial nature as well as his generosity.

In addition to the expert appreciation of the fine arts that his mother had spent nearly twenty years instilling, Will retained his fondness for pranks and jokes as well as a distaste for the regimented, scholastic life. The New England winters he abhorred in prep school continued to affect his disposition throughout his college years. When Will was depressed (which he termed the "dumps" or the "molly grubs"), he found relief in shopping, strolling through art galleries and attending auctions in pursuit of *bibelots* for his burgeoning collections.

Will Hearst wrote screeds of letters to both parents on monogrammed, engraved stationery. To his father he emphasized his academic pursuits and their relevance to his future; his mother was the recipient of detailed health bulletins and constant appeals for supplements to his allowance.

In one of his earliest letters from college to his father, Will wrote

> …a fellow can study or loaf just as he pleases and if he manages to skim through his examinations all right, nothing is said. It is hard to get very high marks at Harvard without regularly "grinding" for the examinations are three hours long, and comprise the work of several months; yet I think a fellow ought to get an average of 70% and that is what I shall try for…. Next year I can choose whatever studies I please and I'll take Spanish and whatever else you wish."[34]

He also wrote to his father at length about campus political activities. Will Hearst considered himself a staunch Democrat during the 1884 Presidential campaign, organizing a forty-member club, "which includes all the democratic dudes in college, and, for a fact, most of the swells are for [Democratic candidate Grover] Cleveland…."[35]

Not surprisingly, Will remained emotionally closer to his mother, conveying his homesickness and general unhappiness with life in New England:

> …I feel very dismal. I had a cold for a few days and then (as I telegraphed) I had the pink eye…. I awake in the morning to find one or both of my eyes closed, and sometimes I am able to open them only by using my hands…. I have had to be very careful—stop smoking altogether, stop reading, except in the early morning, and go to bed at the unreasonable hour of nine o'clock….

> There is but little going on here at present and what little there is doesn't interest me much. I have had the "molly grubs" for the last week or so. I am beginning to get awfully tired of this place and I long to get out West somewhere where I can stretch myself without coming in contact with the narrow walls with which the prejudice of the beaneaters has surrounded us…

> I long to see our own woods, the jagged rocks and towering mountains, the majestic pines, the grand impressive scenery of the "far West." I shall never live anywhere but in California and I like to be away for awhile only to appreciate it the more when I return.

> …Here I am almost busted again before the month is ended. For of the $50 that remained over from what you sent me after everything was paid, twelve dollars went immediately for photographs of my room and the rest has gradually leaked out until now I have only $10 to my name and what I am to do next month when my drug store and livery and my pink-eye doctor bills come in I don't

know. Besides next month I will have to [have] tutor[ing] a little—I hope a very little—and this will take still more money and then there will be a farewell dinner or two. Oh, my, Harvard is no place for a poor boy.

…I know that I may have to work my way in the world and… I do not feel terrified at the prospect, although, of course, I should prefer to have enough money to be able to turn my time to politics or science or something where I could make a name.[36]

An increasingly busy social life, on and off campus, did nothing to reconcile Hearst to the rigors of both the Harvard curriculum and Massachusetts winters. His scholastic status continued to slide, primarily because of his absence from the classroom rather than any difficulty with the curriculum. His increasing admiration for the theatre led him to join the Hasty Pudding Club. Of his acceptance into this group, he wrote, "I had a very pleasant time running for the club and didn't have to do anything but sing and dance and say my temperance speech. I met a great many nice fellows who treated me very kindly…."[37]

Will's birthday in April, 1884, again found him in "the dumps today and I feel rather homesick and I wish I could enjoy my birthday at home and with you and father instead of with a lot of fellows who don't care whether I am twenty-one or thirty so long as the dinner is good and the wine is plenty."[38]

Will's interest in politics, the theatre, and art collecting grew, but his ability to live within his allowance did not, as his frequent letters to his mother attest:

> I hate to talk about money in my letters. You think I'm so mercenary, but my doctor's bills! oh! those doctor's bills! Oliver I owe $50.00. The Springfield doctor $30. And the Cambridge doctor marks at present $18, but is steadily rising. Every sneeze costs somewhere between fifty cents and one dollar…
>
> By the way, I have just bought for you that "de luxe" Thackeray which was worth three or four hundred dollars. Paid one ninety for it. G.B.—great bargain….
>
> I suppose we can afford to indulge our aesthetic tastes now that the [San Francisco] house is sold and Pa is flush. It almost breaks my heart to have our home go and…even some of our lovely furniture will have to follow. Really I should have objected to that…. And since the house is sold, Vive la [Pleasanton] ranch! Now we must get Mr. Briggs' brother, who is a young architect of considerable reputation, to plan us a $25,000

William Randolph Hearst (right) with a friend during his college days at Harvard.

house to be erected upon our estate in the country, don't ye know. And now to wind up a customary plea. Give me one penny for bread. That is to say send me a few dollars to defray expenses of a club life…[39]

Shortly after his senior year began in the fall of 1885, the dean brought Hearst up short, noting Will's chronic absence from the classroom and his failure to take several make-up tests. The bad news was sent to Phoebe by wire:

> SAW THE DEAN, REQUESTED NOT TO RETURN. SAW THE PRESIDENT, SAID IF I WENT TO A GOOD CLIMATE AND STUDIED WITH A COMPETENT INSTRUCTOR, I SHOULD PROBABLY BE ALLOWED TO PASS MY EXAMINATIONS IN JUNE.[40]

Not surprisingly, Phoebe Hearst was the only member of the family upset by his academic difficulties. She hurried to the East Coast to begin the familiar process of hiring tutors, who would then plan a course of study that would reopen Harvard's doors to Will. Clearly Will was not disturbed by his suspension. His coursework had never inspired any sustained application of his intelligence. A fellow student summed up Hearst's attitude succinctly by noting he was a student of "amiable indolence broken by spasms of energy."[41] Perhaps the most significant "spasm of energy" was Hearst's stint as business manager of the Harvard

Lampoon the previous spring. The campus humor magazine had never been operated profitably, relying instead upon student members of the staff who were wealthy enough to make up any deficits out of their own pockets. Eugene Lent had originally been named to the post of business manager, but his allowance, unlike Hearst's, was not generous enough to meet the *Lampoon*'s financial needs.

An offer was made to Hearst to co-manage the "sheet" with his friend, which he accepted. But instead of simply telegraphing home for additional funds from the seemingly bottomless Hearst fortune, he proposed to untangle the *Lampoon*'s financial morass directly, running the magazine as a business. Proud of his considerable efforts, he wrote his mother:

> …[I] spend all my spare time in "booming" the "Lampoon"…. Eugene and I…drum up subscriptions and advertisements, keep the books, send the exchanges and attend to all the business of the paper…. We scoured the country for ads, we ransacked the college for subscriptions, in fact we infused energy into the Lampoon and now we stand on a firm basis with a subscription list of 450 and $900 in advertising, making a grand total of $2250 and leaving $650 clear profit after the debt is paid.

> Show this to Papa and tell him just to wait till Gene and I get hold of the old Examiner and we'll boom her in the same way—she needs it. I am

going to send out a lot of <u>Lampoons</u> and circulars in a few days, and I would like you to get the names of the Harvard Club men and send them each a copy and a circular.[42]

At the time of his academic suspension, Hearst wrote to his father of a future career in "law, politics or journalism, and under favorable circumstances it might be possible to combine all three." That made Washington the ideal place to serve out his suspension, with "opportunities of hearing the debates in Congress, familiarizing myself with legislative methods of procedure, and thus at once assisting my present college studies and preparing the way for a brilliant entree into the political arena, some time in the future."[43]

In mid-March of 1886 George joined his wife and son in Washington. Senator John Miller had died in office and George Hearst was appointed by California Governor George Stoneman to fill the seat until a replacement was elected on July 3, 1886. Phoebe found a suitably impressive house in the Capitol at 1400 New Hampshire Avenue, N.W. and began to recreate the successes of her San Francisco salon. She and Will also availed themselves of the cultural resources of the city. California's newest senator filled his days with politicking, despite his discomfort in the frock coat he was now compelled to wear. He particularly enjoyed the camaraderie of his fellow

senator, railroad baron Leland Stanford. George Hearst was elected in his own right to a six-year term in the Senate, beginning in March of 1887.

Although he attended to his tutors that winter, Will spent more time studying New York, Boston, and Washington daily papers, forming strong opinions about what he found successful or wanting in each paper. Hearst most admired Joseph Pulitzer's New York *World*, a working-class publication that offered readers a mélange of news laced with scandal, gossip, and sensation.

Will wrote again to his father, this time expressing direct hopes for a journalistic career. His passionately worded letter reveals an energy and capacity for detail completely missing from his academic work:

George Hearst served in the U. S. Senate from 1886 to 1891.

I have just finished and dispatched a letter to the Editor of the Examiner... comment[ing] on the illustrations, if you may call them such, which have lately disfigured the paper. ...The cuts that have recently appeared in the paper bore an unquestionable resemblance to the Cuticura Soap advertisements; and I ...believe that our editor has illustrated many of his articles from his stock on hand of cuts representing gentlemen before and after using that efficacious remedy.

...Let me beg of you to remonstrate with him and thus prevent him from giving the finishing stroke to our miserable little sheet. ...I am convinced that I could run a newspaper successfully. Now if you should make over to me the Examiner, with enough money to carry out my schemes, I'll tell you what I would do.

In the first place I would change the general appearance of the paper and make seven wide columns where we now have nine narrow ones, then I would have the type spaced more, and these two changes would give the pages a much cleaner and neater appearance.

Secondly, it would be well to make the paper as far as possible original... and to imitate only some such leading journal as the New York World which is undoubtedly the best paper of that class to which the Examiner belongs—that class which appeals to the people and which depends for its success upon enterprise, energy and a certain startling originality and not upon the wisdom of its political opinions or the lofty style of its editorials....

Thirdly, we must advertise the paper from Oregon to New Mexico and must also increase our number of advertisements if we have to lower our rates to do it....

Illustrations embellish a page; illustrations attract the eye and stimulate the imagination of the lower classes and materially aid the comprehension of an unaccustomed reader and thus are of particular importance to that class of people which the Examiner claims to address....

And now to close with a suggestion of great consequences, namely, that all these changes be made not by degrees but at once so that the improvement will be very marked and noticeable and will attract universal attention and comment....

Well goodbye. I have given up all hope of having you write to me, so I suppose I must just scratch along and trust to hearing of you through the newspapers. By the way, I heard you had bought 2000 acres of land the other day and I hope some of it was the land adjoining our [San Simeon]ranch that I begged you to buy in my last letter.[44]

Though the letter made plain Will's desire for a career in newspapers, it seems everyone in the family had conflicting ideas about what future path William Randolph Hearst should take. His mother continued to opt for higher education; George hoped to interest him in the management of the family's land and mining properties.

In May of 1886, Will petitioned Harvard, asking permission to take his final examinations. Far from being upset, Will was more than happy to sever his relations with the college. He wrote to his mother: "I don't propose to eat any more crow myself nor to serve any to the rest of the family so if you please we will proceed with the next course…. I assured the gentlemen of the Faculty of Harvard College," he continued, "that I didn't regret so much having lost my degree as having given them an opportunity to refuse it to me."[45]

At his father's request, Will began a series of trips with college friend Jack Follansbee to visit various Hearst-owned enterprises. Records detailing his activities during this year are varied, but it is evident that William Randolph Hearst matured appreciably. Instead of the letters from college that rationalized his poor attendance record and poorer marks, Hearst began to send (especially to his father) letters that reveal not only his growing interest in journalism, but also his organizational and analytical skills.

Despite the tour of duty at family-owned enterprises, Will retained his original enthusiasm for the newspaper business in general and the San Francisco *Examiner* in particular. Although George remained unconvinced that journalism was a suitable career, he eventually relented and deeded ownership of the newspaper to his son, together with the funds to make up the paper's deficits.

William Randolph Hearst's response to his father was one of even greater enthusiasm and sense of purpose. He wrote:

> …I am anxious to begin work on the Examiner. I have all the pipes laid, and it only remains to turn on the gas…. We must be alarmingly enterprising, and we must be startlingly original. We must be honest and fearless. We must have greater variety than we have ever had…. There are some things that I intend to do new and striking which will constitute a revolution in the sleepy journalism of the Pacific slope…[46]

On the same day George Hearst was sworn into office as a United States Senator from California, his son began a sixty-four year career in journalism with an inconspicuous announcement on an inside page of the March 4, 1887, issue of the San Francisco paper:

> The *Examiner*, with this issue, has become the exclusive property of William R. Hearst, son of its former proprietor. It will be conducted in future on the same lines and policies which characterized its career under the control of Senator Hearst.[47]

This modest notice on an inside page of the San Francisco Examiner *on March 4, 1887, heralded the beginning of William Randolph Hearst's long career in journalism.*

THE EXAMINER has made a big strike by effecting an arrangement with the New York Herald to have all the Herald's cable news from Europe telegraphed to the EXAMINER.—N. Y. Times Prime.

THE SAN FRANCISCO EXAMINER has secured the exclusive right of foreign dispatches to the New York Herald by the Mackay-Bennett cable, they appearing simultaneously in the Herald and EXAMINER.—Grass Valley Union.

The Daily Examiner.

NO. 63.

SAN FRANCISCO: FRIDAY MORNING, MARCH 4, 1887—SIX-PAGE EDITION.

VOL. XLIV.

THE REICHSTAG.

Formal Opening of the Imperial German Parliament.

The Stately and Magnificent Ceremony.

The Reading of the Emperor William's Address.

It Is Received with Favor and Even Enthusiasm.

The Veteran Von Moltke the Recipient of Marked Honors.

THE JUBILEE YEAR.

The First Splendid Court Festival at Buckingham Palace.

Greater Attendance Than Ever Before Known.

American Youth, Beauty and Wealth Out in Full Force.

Resplendently Adorned With Bewitching Toilets.

RAILROAD CONNUBIATION.

A Banquet at Baltimore That Has Alarmed Wall Street.

Magnates in Council Discuss the Interstate Law.

THE LABOR UNITY.

A Report Written and Sent to Rome on the Knights of Labor.

By Monsignor Straniero, Late Papal Abligate.

Based on What He Saw When He Visited the United States.

The Principles and Objects of the Order Fairly Stated.

Most Valuable Testimony from a Trustworthy Source.

THE KNIGHTS OF LABOR.

HAPLESS BABES.

More Tales of Cowardly Cruelty Toward Helpless Victims.

Physicians Who Aid in Murder

For the Sake of Receiving a Paltry Fee.

Infants Purposely Mangled At Their Birth,

And Willfully Exposed to Death from Cold.

A DEADLY FEUD.

The Fierce Warfare Between Coronado and Leoti, Kan.

Hostilities Renewed and a Reign of Terror Begun.

CHAPTER TWO

The World of Journalism

William Randolph Hearst was not a journalistic innovator. Rather, Hearst's genius lay in skillfully adapting the innovations of others to his own purposes. His only innovation, and it was a considerable one, lay in the fact that he could take a new idea and put it into practice in a bigger and better way than the originator had ever conceived.

Hearst arrived on the journalistic scene at a time of unprecedented change. During the period from 1880 to 1890, newspapers serving large urban areas were growing at a phenomenal pace, partly because Americans were moving from rural areas to cities in record numbers. Increasing numbers of European immigrants also contributed to the booming urban population.

The proliferation of newspapers also owed a great deal to recent technological advances. Newspapers reached their destinations more quickly because of improved transportation. News-gathering was aided immeasurably by the use of the telephone, the telegraph, and the beginning of wire services that provided dispatches from remote locations. Newsprint was manufactured more rapidly and at less expense with the advent of wood-pulp papermaking processes. High-speed printing was made possible by multi-page presses and Linotype.

But the greatest change at the time William Randolph Hearst entered the field was in the people who read newspapers. For new city dwellers arriving from farms or foreign countries, "the daily newspaper was the

Front page of The Daily Examiner *the day W. R. Hearst became proprietor.*

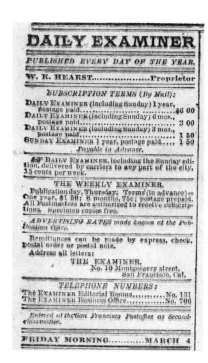

With the financial support of his parents, W. R. Hearst was able to increase the size of his first paper, yet reduce the cost for subscribers.

chronicler of the national scene and interpreter of the new environment."[1]

Two more critical factors explain the growth in newspapers during this period. The literacy rate doubled in the last thirty years of the nineteenth century while the workweek declined by nearly ten hours between 1850 and 1900. This increase in leisure time spurred the growth of newspapers and created the demand for new methods of entertainment and communication, including national magazines, newsreels, and motion pictures.

The circulation of daily newspapers increased 400 percent between 1870 and 1900, while the nation's population grew by 95 percent. The most successful urban newspaper publishers were those who shrewdly assessed their new audiences and published their papers accordingly. Joseph Pulitzer's *World*, which had fueled Hearst's interest in the business, was the model for the new urban newspaper with a large and growing circulation. The articles published had entertainment value as well as news content. They not only commanded attention, they were also easy to read. Publishers began to target their audiences, deliberately creating sections and features that appealed to specific groups, including women, professionals, children, hobbyists, and sports enthusiasts. The results of investigative reporting and crusades that championed the working classes were given prominent space.[2]

Hearst plunged into every aspect of his new business. He arranged for the San Francisco *Examiner* to share the foreign news sent by Mackay-Bennet cable with the New York *Herald*. The first issue of the *Examiner* under his leadership featured headlines about Queen Victoria's Golden Jubilee and the opening of Germany's Parliament by Kaiser Wilhelm. News about labor unions from various parts of the country jostled side by side with an article exposing conditions at a children's hospital in San Francisco:

HAPLESS BABES…

COWARDLY CRUELTY TOWARD

HELPLESS VICTIMS

PHYSICIANS AID IN MURDER

FOR THE SAKE OF RECEIVING A PALTRY FEE

In less than a month, Hearst had a momentous regional event upon which to capitalize: the Del Monte Hotel in Monterey had gone up in flames. The elaborate resort hotel, built by railroad magnate Charles Crocker, had become very popular with San Francisco's elite. Hearst himself had spent many happy summer holidays at the Del Monte. His reaction to this event typified his entire career. Though he did not scoop the other newspapers in San Francisco, he did provide the most thorough coverage using unprecedented methods. He wrote the first two-column wide headlines on the event himself:

HUNGRY, FRANTIC FLAMES
"LEAPING HIGHER, HIGHER, HIGHER,
WITH DESPERATE DESIRE"
RUNNING MADLY RIOTOUS
THROUGH CORNICE, ARCHWAY AND FACADE.
RUSHING IN UPON THE TREMBLING GUESTS
WITH SAVAGE FURY[3]

Most San Francisco newspapers, including Hearst's principal rivals, the *Chronicle* and the *Call*, waited in San Francisco for further reports to come in over the telegraph. Such passivity would never do for Hearst, who chartered a special train to Monterey so that his reporters could file datelines from the actual scene of the fire. One writer deemed it "an act of competitive aggressiveness unheard of in journalism on the Pacific Slope. 'Are the wires down?' asked a gentleman in amazement as the *Examiner* train stopped in Menlo Park to cool the hot box. 'No, they are not sufficient,' was the Hearstian reply."[4]

In the following day's edition, the *Examiner* editorial staff congratulated the *Examiner* reporters on fine coverage of the Del Monte Hotel blaze, beginning the long and unceasing practice of Hearst publications praising themselves. Though Will had been considered a convivial fellow at Harvard, he was also thought to be quite shy. This personal reticence was never carried over to the newspapers or other hold-

ings that became a part of the Hearst empire. The *Examiner* was self-christened "Monarch of the Dailies," to which was later added the all-embracing "Supreme in Everything."

Fueled by prodigious amounts of his time and his family's money, the newspaper began to attract attention and circulation slowly began to build. Early in 1887 Hearst wrote to his mother of his absorption in his new career:

This sketch of the young editor of the San Francisco Examiner *was published in northern California and provided welcome publicity for Hearst, as well as his newspaper.*

…I don't suppose I will live more than two or three weeks if this strain keeps up. I don't get to bed until about two o'clock and I wake up at about seven in the morning and can't get to sleep again, for I must see the paper and compare it with the <u>Chronicle</u>. If we are the best I can turn over and go to sleep with quiet satisfaction but if the <u>Chronicle</u> happens to scoop us, that lets me out of all sleep for the day.

The newspaper business is no fun and I had no idea quite how hard a job I was undertaking when I entered upon the editorial management of the <u>Examiner</u>….The great and good people of California want the <u>Examiner</u>. They don't want it very bad; they don't want it much harder than at the rate of about thirty additional copies a day, but in time this will count and if we can manage to keep ahead we will have in a year from thirty to thirty-two thousand subscribers. That will put us away ahead of the Call and well up with the Chronicle.[5]

Hearst turned his attention to the equipment with which the paper was produced, which consisted of an antiquated web press and two telephones housed in a rented building. Before the year was out, he was scouring the country, visiting newspaper offices to inspect their presses and appraise their staff. He sent his father a barrage of letters, broadly hinting at the need to purchase the most sophisticated twelve-page presses.

Hearst also began a vigorous housecleaning of inherited staff members who had not been able to keep up with his changes. New editors, illustrators, and writers were hired, including his childhood friend, Eugene Lent, who wrote for the financial and society sections, as well as Frank Noble, Ernest Lawrence Thayer (who would later write "Casey at the Bat"), and Fred Briggs, all of whom had worked with him on the Harvard *Lampoon*.

He began to search for a new managing editor for the *Examiner*, hoping to find someone who would share his perfervid philosophy of journalism while handling the day-to-day business of guiding the other editors and staff members. The search was often discouraging, for few individuals could keep pace with Hearst's

grand philosophy and ambitious plans. These depressions were temporary, for Hearst usually managed to lift his spirits by borrowing the circulation-boosting new ideas of rival papers. His search for a managing editor eventually ended on the East Coast when he met Sam Chamberlain, "a tall, urbane individual, a veteran newspaper reporter whose bouts with the bottle were widely spaced but determined."[6]

Another important addition to Hearst's staff was editorialist Arthur McEwen, whose philosophy of journalism was clear. "Gee-whiz" was the reaction McEwen wanted from readers on the first page. The second page McEwen thought readers should cry, "Holy Moses!" and by the third page they should leap from their chairs, shouting, "God Almighty!"[7]

In 1887, the *Chronicle*'s owner, M.H. de Young, decided to build a large, permanent building for his newspaper's operation. Once Hearst heard of the plan, he was unsatisfied with the *Examiner*'s plebian rented building. He began an immediate campaign to his father for a larger, grander *Examiner* building, imploring:

> Whether or not we like Mr. de Young's building, it is considered remarkably fine by everybody here. He is going to put in his tower the largest clock face in the world. These clock faces will front to the four points of the compass, will be lighted by electricity and will be visible all

over San Francisco and from Oakland. I didn't believe this when I was told it but I went across the bay and found that it was so. The tower can be seen distinctly now and when it is all lit up with electricity it will be simply tremendous. The entrances…will be finished in white marble and when these too are lit up with electricity it will be pretty dazzling and don't you forget it…

Of course friends of ours say the <u>Examiner</u> is going to put up a building too but they can't be saying that [forever]. The <u>Examiner</u> has been successful not because it has been going to do something in the future but because it has been doing something in the present all the time. Now we are losing subscribers, we are losing advertisements, we are losing prestige…

You will have to do just as de Young has done. You have got to put a million or a million and a half or two million dollars into it…[8]

Hearst's *Examiner* building, which would not become a reality for nearly six years, was the first of many building projects—and underscored his conviction that he must always outdo his competitors.

Hearst also prized well-known writers, whose marquee value was as important as their talent. Journalist and critic Ambrose Bierce, one of California's literary lions, recalled being interrupted in his office at the San Francisco *Argonaut*: " 'I am from the San Francisco *Examiner*,' he explained in a voice like the fragrance of violets made audible, and backed a little away. 'Oh,' I said, 'you come from Mr. Hearst?' Then that unearthly child lifted his blue eyes and cooed, 'I am Mr. Hearst.' "[9]

A munificent salary induced Bierce to join the *Examiner*, where his acidulous pen was employed in columns and features commenting upon the events of the day. Bierce delivered scathing judgments on virtually any topic in his Sunday column, "The Passing Show: A Record of Personal Opinion and Dissent," which kept Hearst's attorneys on the defensive. Hearst was impressed with Bierce, who would remain with Hearst newspapers for twenty years, though he resigned and was immediately rehired with almost clockwork regularity. Bierce led a number of crusades launched by Hearst, from reduced water rates in San Francisco, to American intervention in Cuba, to the attempt to "bust the railroad trust."

The Southern Pacific Railroad was a monolithic economic force in the West, using its power to condemn land for right-of-way, making or breaking towns in its path, and maintaining high rates for shipping and freight. Bierce,

New York architects Kirby, Petit, and Green designed the new Hearst building in 1911, replacing the original building that was destroyed in the San Francisco earthquake and fire.

The Examiner *building at Third and Market Streets in San Francisco.*

Jack London, and Winifred Sweet, one of the first "sob-sister" reporters. Hearst was inspired by Pulitzer's Nellie Bly, who did not wait for news to report, but created it. Her most famous exploit was her trip around the world, attempting to best the eighty days it had taken Jules Verne's fictional character, Phileas Fogg. Succeeding in only seventy-two days, Bly and her trip were featured on the front page for several months, boosting the *World*'s circulation to dizzying heights.

Winifred Sweet began her career in 1889 as a $15-per-week reporter for Hearst's paper, using "Annie Laurie" as her sob-sister pseudonym. She was pigeonholed for a time by the limited imagination of male editors who felt the only topics suitable for women reporters were society parties and charity bazaars. Eventually Annie Laurie became an integral contributor to the *Examiner*, combining "created" news and the exposé, two time-tested Hearstian methods.

Editor Sam Chamberlain chose her first topic: medical treatment for the indigent. Laurie had her doctor place belladonna drops in her eyes to achieve an authentic glaze. Dressed in shabby clothes with job advertisements stuffed in her pockets and handbag, she walked up and down Kearny Street several times before collapsing on the pavement. Her realistic acting attracted a crowd of concerned San Franciscans, who in turn summoned police. The two

whose umbrage against the S.P. was already well known, noted in one issue that Southern Pacific's trains were habitually so late, they exposed passengers "to the perils of senility."[10] Though the *Examiner*'s crusade against "the octopus" gained subscriptions for the newspaper, it had little immediate impact on the operating policies of the Southern Pacific Railroad. Eventually, however, the congressional subsidies the railroad demanded were voted down, a product of the "trust-busting" mood that had developed nationally.

Hearst's reputation for offering generous salaries quickly provided him with an experienced staff. In addition to Bierce, his writers in San Francisco included Mark Twain, Gertrude Atherton, Bret Harte, Joaquin Miller, police officers assumed she was drunk, despite the fact that there was no whiskey on her breath. "I wish I could say the same for you," the reporter thought, but did not say.[11]

The officer ordered an unsprung prison wagon and unceremoniously shoved her aboard for the jolting journey over rough cobblestones to the city hospital, where the physician on duty administered the standard treatment: a forced dosing of an emetic and a quick trip back onto the street.

Laurie's rousing account of her treatment in the next day's *Examiner* resulted in the suspension of the doctor, re-evaluation of hospital staff, and the purchase of the city's first ambulance. The article also brought the guilty physician to the *Examiner*'s offices in a towering rage. According to the next day's paper (for this event was duly reported as well), a reporter landed a punch on the doctor, who "lay on his back whining like a whipped cur."[12]

Subsequent stories filed by Annie Laurie documented her experiences posing as a Mormon in polygamous Utah, a Salvation Army lassie on the vice-ridden Barbary Coast, a low-paid seasonal worker at an unsafe fruit cannery, a naive consumer of quack cures and unsafe cosmetics, and an unskilled laborer at an exploitative cotton mill in the South. She also covered such diverse subjects as the leper colony on Molokai ("the saddest place on earth"), a prizefight, a whore-house, and the overcrowded Children's Hospital in San Francisco.

She first inspired the sobriquet "sob sister" when covering the Harry Thaw trial in 1907. Thaw had murdered architect Stanford White because of his affair with Evelyn Nesbit, Thaw's wife. Nesbit received a great deal of blame and abuse in the press, but Laurie and three other female reporters were sympathetic to her and said so in their articles. Thus the tag that Laurie came to detest, however successful. In time, other female reporters would duplicate Laurie's success, until the sob sister became a requisite member of every newspaper's staff.

The Hearst technique of arousing public sympathy with a mixture of sentiment and idealism proved to be a tremendous circulation booster when practiced by reporters of either gender. Male reporters for Hearst did not write under pseudonyms, but they did undertake similar adventures in "created news." One of Hearst's own favorites was the rescue of several fishermen who had suffered an accident on a stormy day just outside the Golden Gate. The weather and failing daylight prevented the launching of a rescue party. The fishermen were last seen clinging to a rock, where it was doubted that they could remain until sunrise and rescue.

Bierce and eight other staff members speculated on their fate while determining that the story deserved front-page space. But the group decided

Phoebe Apperson Hearst and William Randolph Hearst at the family's country house near Pleasanton, California.

Well into his second year of publishing, Hearst showed no signs of disenchantment with his chosen profession. He kept his father and mother, who had both made substantial financial contributions to the paper, apprised of his progress. Hearst also appealed to his father to use his influence on the *Examiner*'s behalf, seizing every tool available to insure the success of his newspaper. In mid-1888, Hearst wrote to his father:

> …Papa, you must do your best for us and you must do it immediately. Delay would be as fatal as neglect.
>
> First see Senator [Leland] Stanford and try to get him interested in the progress of the paper. A man like Senator Stanford ought to feel some interest in a paper whose object is to do the right thing, the strong thing and the best thing by the people of the coast. He will know that our paper will be honest and pure and that it will never be guilty of any blackmailing schemes or filthy transactions…
>
> If we can get Senator Stanford to take an interest in the prosperity of our paper the greatest stroke towards its success will have been made.
>
> At present the news companies on the trains—especially the S.P.—discriminate against the <u>Examiner</u> for the benefit of the <u>Chronicle</u>. We receive letters constantly saying that they can't get <u>Examiners</u> on the train and coming home I had a conversation with one of the news boys on the train and he said that

they were not content with merely reporting the story and left for the waterfront, where an ocean-going tug was leased at the paper's expense. A dramatic rescue was effected, involving a Hearst reporter who jumped into the sea secured by a rope around his waist to reach the stranded fishermen. Hearst's joy was unalloyed, for not only had the men's lives been saved, but the *Examiner* had also scored a coup. Hearst recalled that his paper

> came out an hour or so later with pictures, and a full account of the exploit, spread all over the first page… The other papers appeared with a dismal story of how the ill-fated fishermen had been abandoned as lost.[13]

the news company only gave him fifteen Examiners but that he could sell fifty.[14]

So blind was Hearst's determination to succeed that it apparently never occurred to him Leland Stanford was not pleased about the *Examiner*'s relentless criticism of Stanford's own railroad, the Southern Pacific.

Hearst was also blind to the amount of money he was constantly drawing upon for his newspaper's success. Phoebe, however, had kept track of the figures, sending the following summary to George:

> From Aug /87 to Aug /88 Will has spent forty seven thousand-nine hundred and thirty-nine dollars. This is his [personal] account, then the amount drawn for the Examiner is one hundred & eighty four thousand five hundred & thirteen dollars, making a very large sum."[15]

By the end of that year, the Hearsts came to a joint decision that their liberal financial support of their son's newspaper must stop.

When Will asked for an additional $50,000 for unspecified expenses, both of his parents refused to advance the sum, disappointed that their son could not practice economic restraint, though they had never taught it. Hearst was desperate, believing that he would lose the paper after nearly two years of constant labor. He appealed to Michael Francis Tarpey, the Democratic National Committee Chair from Califor-

nia, who also happened to be an old friend of George's from the early days of the California gold rush. Tarpey reassured Will that the funds would be forthcoming from his father. "We were in the heat of a campaign," Tarpey recalled.

> I went to the Senator and told him that the party needed contributions, and he was down for one hundred thousand dollars for the Democratic cause. The Senator didn't hesitate. I received his check for that amount. Half of the sum went into our campaign fund. The other fifty thousand dollars I turned over to young William for his and the paper's espousal of the Democratic principles. I do not know that Will ever required any more money for his paper. It soon became an outstanding and successful journal.[16]

Eventually George Hearst relented and continued to help the *Examiner* directly, for the newspaper was not solvent until 1890.

By that time, George Hearst was in declining health. Though proud of his son's achievements, he remained disappointed that Will had not decided to join him in the management of the family's holdings. George was also upset that his son continued to spend profligate sums of the family's money personally, most notably the purchase of art objects.

On February 28, 1891, George Hearst died at his Washington, D.C., residence, with Phoebe, Will, Jack

Follansbee, and his physician at his bedside. The San Francisco *Examiner* devoted the whole front page, bordered in black, to the Senator's career. The *New York Times* obituary was headlined:

DEATH OF SENATOR HEARST

END OF A CAREER WHICH WAS PHENOMENAL.

FROM AN ILLITERATE PENNILESS GOLD

HUNTER TO A POPULAR MEMBER OF THE

NATIONAL LEGISTLATURE AND A MILLIONAIRE.

The *Times* devoted two columns to his obituary, remembering George Hearst as "a kind-hearted man, lavish with his expenditures for the relief of the poor; and it is said that he never forgot his old friends." Said a correspondent to the *Times* in 1886: "I have personally seen him on more than one occasion leave a party of broad-clothed men to step across the street and shake hands with some ragged wreck of a pioneer whom he had known in the early days." He was also a convivial fellow and, as one of his friends once put it, took his conviviality "straight," and could stand a great deal of it.[17]

George Hearst left his entire estate, including eighteen million dollars in cash, directly to his wife, continuing W.R.'s dependence upon his mother to finance his business and personal life.

Deeply wounded that his father so obviously refused to trust his judgment about money, Hearst vowed to practice economy—but soon began planning another trip to Europe to buy art. He also started construction of the long-awaited, custom-designed *Examiner* building. In 1893, after the move into the new building was completed, Will wrote an importunate letter to his mother, requesting a change in the handling of financial matters that would finally recognize him, at the age of 30, as an adult. He wrote:

The request I make would not amount to an increase of my salary so much as a change of the manner of delivering it. I beg of you to instruct Mr. Stump [the Hearst family's financial manager] to put to my credit at any bank on the first of each month a definite sum of $2500.

…First, I think I might properly have now what was doubtless too much for me three years ago.

Secondly, I should be very happy to be relieved of the inconvenience of dealing with Stump on an indefinite basis. As long as I come to ask him for extra thousand dollars here and there, he will treat me as a child asking ten cents for soda water. "Can't you get along with five cents?" "Soda water isn't very good for you anyhow." "Well come around next month and I will talk to you about it."

There is mixed with [Stump's] patronage an air of business mistrustfulness such as you might meet at a bank where you were overdrawing your account. This is annoying but it is unavoidable under the present system…

Now positively I will, from the moment this new arrangement goes into effect, lay aside, not to spend but to invest one half of all income from the paper, the ranch and all property that I may have or acquire. Reports of my business can go through Mr. Stump's hands and my books will be at his command so that he can see that I am faithfully carrying out my part of the plan.

…I shall feel satisfied with [this] arrangement and will not demand or desire any extra money. I will not be asking you for a thousand dollars on Christmas, a thousand on my birthday, a thousand for Bell, a thousand now and then for unforeseen expenses. I give you my word to this. I can get along with that amount and will without any requests for extra money…

You have always been most kind and generous to me and have given me extra money whenever I asked for it but don't you think it would be better for me if I didn't ask for it so often,—if I were put now on a more independent and manly footing?[18]

Phoebe decided to sell her shares in the Anaconda mines, conferring $7.5 million on her son from the proceeds. While he was never able to manage his finances as he promised in the letter to his mother, the proceeds from the Anaconda sale had secured for him a measure of financial independence. Without hesitation, he decided to enter the newspaper market in New York City, where he would compete directly with Joseph Pulitzer's *World*, the paper that had not only sparked his interest in publishing, but also provided the model

for his success in San Francisco.

The New York paper Hearst chose to buy was John McLean's *Journal*, a morning publication. At the time of McLean's purchase in 1894 the paper was described as the "chambermaids' delight." McLean had purchased it for $1 million from Joseph Pulitzer's brother, Alfred, attempting to turn the paper into a political powerhouse. He was successful only in driving away the original working-class readers, for its circulation had dropped to only 77,000 readers when he sold the paper to Hearst in September of 1895 for the bargain price of $180,000. Hearst did not publicly announce ownership of the paper until November 8 of that year.[19]

One of Hearst's first moves was to drop the price to a penny an issue while expanding the paper to sixteen sheets, a feat that would have been fiscally impossible without the Hearst fortune behind him. Pulitzer was unconcerned, for his paper had large-circulation morning, evening, and Sunday editions selling at two cents apiece and advertising revenue that far outstripped the nearly moribund *Journal*.

In less than six months, Pulitzer was forced to pay attention to the Western newcomer at the *Journal*, for Hearst was using the well-proven methods of the new urban journalism. The working classes were courted with scare head-

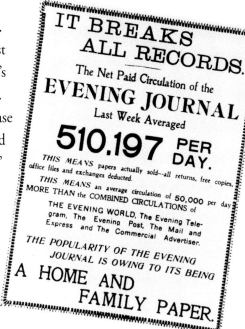

IT BREAKS ALL RECORDS.

The Net Paid Circulation of the

EVENING JOURNAL

Last Week Averaged

510,197 PER DAY.

THIS MEANS papers actually sold--all returns, free copies, office files and exchanges deducted.

THIS MEANS an average circulation of 50,000 per day MORE THAN the COMBINED CIRCULATIONS of THE EVENING WORLD, The Evening Telegram, The Evening Post, The Mail and Express and The Commercial Advertiser.

THE POPULARITY OF THE EVENING JOURNAL IS OWING TO ITS BEING

A HOME AND FAMILY PAPER.

The New York Journal *was Hearst's first business venture outside his native California and a success in less than six months.*

lines, sensational news stories, easy-to-read features, "created" news and exposés, and the Hearst self-publicizing policy.

One of Hearst's first hires was a "sob-sister" reporter, who filed the following story on a coal mine disaster:

> I sobbed my way through the line of [bystanders who] stood aside to let me pass with a muttered, "The lady is from the Journal; let her by." I was the first to reach the wounded and the dying. "God bless Mr. Hearst," cried a little child as I stooped to lave her brow; and then she smiled and died. I spread one of our comic supplements over the pale, still face and went on to distribute Mr. Hearst's generous bounty.[20]

Hearst was not only playing Pulitzer's game, but beating him at it. In the first six months of competition, the Journal's circulation had more than doubled, exceeding the 150,000 mark. This figure was uncomfortably close to the World's much-touted 200,000 circulation rate.

Pulitzer was a wealthy eccentric who ran his newspaper not from a publisher's customary lofty office, but from an oceangoing yacht, the Liberty, that traveled the Eastern seaboard. An invalid suffering from a variety of neuroses, Pulitzer was a self-made man who made his fortune in journalism. He was said to have entered his New York newspaper building only once, preferring to do his business by telegraph and correspondence. Despite the state of his health, he was in constant communication with his staff. Though his newspaper employees did not see him, they certainly saw the results of Pulitzer's fanatical attention to detail in his newspaper. The telegraphic business was often conducted in code to foil spies in the publishing industry who Pulitzer was convinced were monitoring his moves. Hearst's code name was "Gush," reflecting Pulitzer's opinion of the amount of money Hearst spent advancing the Journal.

In addition to improving upon the gimmicks first used in the World, Hearst raided the staff of the rival paper, luring them with the now legendary Hearst-sized salaries. Editor Bill Nye wrote a friend, "I am leaving the World, at an advance of 50 percent on salary, by cracky, and going to the Journal..."[21] Hearst also induced the cartoonist and the drama critic to join his staff, signaling the rest of the New York publishers that he was in deadly earnest about the success of his new paper. Hearst continued to hire away various members of Pulitzer's staff, concentrating upon those whose work he had admired when reading every edition of the World that rolled off of Pulitzer's presses.

Hearst's method of reviewing the content of his own newspapers, which he used for the rest of his career, was quite unorthodox. Harry J. Coleman, who began as a copy boy and rose to the ranks of Hearst executives, described in his memoirs the first time he made a delivery to Hearst's office:

> Hearst suddenly spread the proofs in precise order upon the floor and began a sort of tap dance around and between them. It was a mild, uncostumed combination of Carmen Miranda, a rumba, a Russian dagger dance and the Notre Dame shift, with lively castanet accompaniments produced by his snapping fingers. After I had observed W.R.'s strange dance, I learned it was his customary method of absorbing pictures and productions on newspaper pages. The cadence of it speeded up in tempo [when he was displeased] and slowed down to a strolling rhythm when he approved. Between dances, he scribbled illegible scrawls in longhand on the margins and gave the proofs back to me.[22]

Willis Abbot served as New York editor-in-chief and was nominally responsible for the editorial page. In fact, Abbot, like Chamberlain in San Francisco, had been hired to provide day-to-day continuity. Hearst himself kept careful vigil over the editorials. Abbot recalled:

> [Hearst's] greatest joy in life was to attend the theater, follow it up with a lively supper and, at about 1:30 a.m., turn up at the office full of scintillating ideas and therewith rip my editorial page to pieces. It was always an interesting spectacle to me to watch this young millionaire, usually in irreproachable evening dress, working over the forms, changing a head here, shifting the position of an article there, clamoring always for more pictures and bigger type.[23]

Merrill Goddard, who began working for Pulitzer in 1885 after graduating from Dartmouth, was renowned among New York journalists as the creator of the Sunday supplement. Under Goddard's editorship, the supplement grew in size and importance. Its content was created quite simply, needing only a writer "to revamp the sensations of the week's news in nervous, bawling paragraphs."[24] Articles brimming with scandal, crime, and sex were prominently placed next

Hearst courted newspaper readers with scare headlines, sensational news stories, easy-to-read features, and "created" news

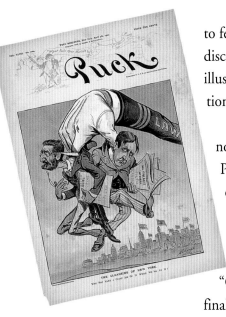

The competition between W. R. Hearst and Joseph Pulitzer frequently landed them on the cover of the era's popular humor magazine, Puck.

to features on bizarre "scientific" discoveries. These pieces were heavily illustrated, though light on documentation.

In January of 1896, Hearst lured not only Goddard, the jewel in Pulitzer's crown, but Goddard's entire staff to the *Journal*. Pulitzer made an immediate counteroffer, which restored his Sunday supplement staff, but only for one day. "Gush" trumped his rival's offer, finally winning Goddard, his staff, and a ready-made Sunday supplement, called the "American Weekly."

The concept reached its sensationalist zenith during Goddard's years with Hearst. Readers whiling away an afternoon with the *Journal*'s Sunday supplement were treated to headlines such as these:

CUTTING A HOLE IN A MAN'S CHEST
TO LOOK AT HIS INTESTINES AND LEAVING
A FLAP THAT WORKS AS IF ON A HINGE

THE SUICIDE OF A HORSE

SCIENCE CAN WASH YOUR HEART[25]

Perhaps the most valued contributor on the Sunday supplement team was Richard Felton Outcault, the artist who is credited as the first Sunday newspaper cartoonist. Thomas Nast and other artists had developed the concept of the political cartoon in daily newspapers and monthly magazines, but Outcault's intentions were strictly humorous. His first offering to Pulitzer was a comic showing a clown and a wolfhound as

chairs. When asked how and why he ventured into the newly developing field of comics, Outcault replied, "I was broke, that's the sum and substance of the whole thing. I was sketching machinery for [inventor Thomas] Edison in Europe," when first struck with the idea.[26] On November 18, 1889, the New York *World* published the first successful Sunday "funny side," consisting of a full newspaper page with the text of a short story describing the events in a single, large color drawing.

In 1895 Outcault created "Hogan's Alley," for the Pulitzer Sunday supplement. One of the background characters was an immigrant boy with a bald head, outsized ears, and large feet, whose name was Johnny Dugan. In the colored strips on Sundays, Dugan was always dressed in a yellow nightshirt. The *World*'s press operator chose yellow for the Kid's outfit after other color schemes failed to print well. The yellow nightshirt "stood out like a sunrise" and Johnny Dugan's popular name was born. Soon, "New York went wild over the Yellow Kid" and Outcault put him in the spotlight.[27]

As other New York publishers were scrambling to capitalize on the idea of the Sunday supplement and the funny side, Outcault drew the Yellow Kid packing his bags and departing "Hogan's Alley" for "McFadden's Row of Flats," his new Hearst home. The term "yellow journalism" came into popular use at this time, symbolizing the sensational tactics Hearst, Pulitzer, and other publishers used in their war for the readership of New York City.

Under Outcault's pen, the format of cartooning changed. Left behind was the one-page, one-drawing format, replaced with the now-traditional series of panels. Balloons that captioned each figure's remarks were borrowed from political cartoons, replacing the need to use the Yellow Kid's generous dress front as the placard for his broken English.

Although the Yellow Kid was a tremendous success, his prominence "gradually subsided because of protests from mothers and preachers. The big-eared moron was the progenitor of American comics in color, but he was not approved of by those who were dubious about the moral effect of the Sunday supplement," according to one historian of journalism.[28] Outcault received an outpouring of mail in response to one Sunday's efforts, which showed the Yellow Kid torching a schoolhouse.

The Yellow Kid's "abnormal impishness" was succeeded seven years later by the pranks of an even more popular Outcault cartoon figure. Buster Brown, an upper-middle-class child, perennially dressed in a foppish sailor suit, provided readers with a safer brand of mischief. Buster's adventures had nothing to do with pyrotechnics; he stayed within more traditional bound-

aries of adventure by visiting his father's office or embarrassing his mother when the local pastor made a house call. Buster was accompanied on each cartoon adventure by his faithful dog, Tige, and, less frequently, by his girlfriend, Mary Jane.

Whatever the scrapes Buster landed in each Sunday, Outcault ended each strip with a "resolution." These homilies typically exhorted his readers to be gentle, considerate, and hardworking, which always led, in Outcault's panels at least, to great reward. Adults and children both followed the Yellow Kid and Buster Brown's antics with great devotion, absorbing the Protestant work ethic that was the philosophical under-pinning of the strip.

Pulitzer and other New York publishers, left without Outcault's services, decided to hire new cartoonists

Cartoonist R. F. Outcault's popular characters for Hearst combined entertainment with hard news during the Spanish-American War.

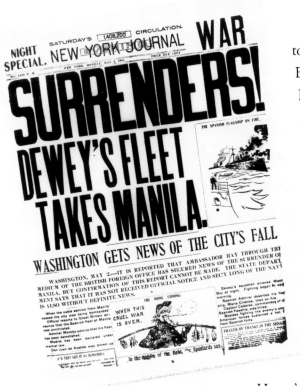

Hearst's New York Journal *reports on the capture of Manila during the Spanish-American War. Hearst trumped Pulitzer by traveling to Cuba personally to report on the war.*

to draw ersatz Buster Browns and Yellow Kids for their newspapers. Soon genuine and imitation Outcault comic strips abounded in the pages of the *World*, the *Journal*, and the *Herald*. Suits and countersuits for copyright infringement were filed, occupying the courts for years to come. Hearst's concern that the imitators would confuse readers led him to run interviews with the cartoon characters in the news section of the *Journal*, under Hearst-inspired headlines:

BUSTER GOES OVER TO HEARST.

COPYRIGHT SUITS IN SIGHT ON

ACCOUNT OF TOW-HEADED YOUNGSTER.

FRIENDS HOPE HE WILL BE GOOD IN COURT[29]

On the first anniversary of his ownership of the New York paper, Hearst revealed his philosophy of journalism in an editorial, "What is the explanation of the *Journal*'s amazing and wholly unmatched progress? It is the *Journal*'s policy to engage brains as well as to get the news, for the public is even more fond of entertainment than it is of information."[30]

While other publishers disliked "yellow journalism," Hearst used the term relentlessly in both of his newspapers, priding himself in practice of "Yellow journalism that yells."[31]

The power of yellow journalism is perhaps best illustrated by America's intervention in the Cuban revolution. Though Hearst is commonly associated with the events that led to the Spanish-American War, the role of Joseph Pulitzer, his very yellow *World*, and the combined circulation battle between them seldom receives equal attention.

The two newspapers were virtually tied in circulation. Pulitzer believed Hearst would spend himself out of business; Hearst believed Pulitzer's precarious emotional state would force him out of competition. "This was the situation," according to W.A. Swanberg, biographer of both men,

> …As the nation's two largest newspaper publishers brought up their siege guns in an attempt to exterminate each other by the cunning use of news. By pure chance it happened that the first big, continuous news issue that came to hand was the revolution in Cuba.[32]

Thus, the journalistic battle between Hearst and Pulitzer for the hearts and minds of New York newspaper readers erupted into a full-scale war in Cuba. Initially, the revolution in Cuba was of little concern to most Americans, but the power of the press brought the conflict home, presenting the rebels as machete-wielding patriots in the tradition of Washington and Jefferson.

Both papers concentrated upon emotional stories featuring sentiment, violence, or a combination of the two. General Valeriano Weyler, sent from Madrid to quell the situation, was described in the *World* as directing the murder of "defenseless, harmless people hiding in their own homes."[33] The Sunday *Journal* gilded their prose, describing Weyler as "the prince of all cruel generals… the fiendish despot whose hand Cuba well knows… hundreds of Cuban women, maids and matrons, shudder."[34]

In the months before American intervention, the *Journal*, the *World*, and the yellow papers "stirred the country to a war psychosis, by not only reporting the events in Cuba, but [also] by making the news."[35] Hearst's reporters freed a Cuban nationalist jailed for trying to save her father's life. Later, the same reporters stole documents from a Spanish diplomatic pouch, and published a letter maligning President McKinley. The newspaper also offered a $50,000 reward for information about the sinking of the U S S *Maine*, and sent an even larger contingent of reporters to Havana to investigate the cause of the explosion.

The competition between the two papers was never far from reporters' minds. Hearst succeeded in greatly embarrassing Pulitzer when his reporters published a phony report on the death of Colonel Reflipe W. Thenuz. The *World* seized the item, rewrote it and placed it in the next edition. The *Journal* then gleefully noted in its next edition that Thenuz did not exist. In fact, the Colonel's name was an anagram for the phrase "We pilfer the news." The *Journal* continued to jibe its rival on the subject for a month.[36]

When war was officially declared in April of 1898, Hearst himself led a group of twenty reporters, including college friend Jack Follansbee, to the front. Hearst filed his own dispatches, covering the Rough Riders' charge up San Juan Hill, the capture of Santiago, and other events. To his mother, who was predictably concerned for his safety, he wrote:

> I am at the front and absolutely safe, so don't worry. [General Garcia] said the <u>Journal</u> had been the most potent influence in bringing the United States to the help of Cuba and they would always remember the <u>Journal</u> as a friend when friends had been very few.
>
> I have been greatly interested in everything and of some service to the hospital ship providing them with ice and delicacies which they lacked.

Pulitzer's New York World *also reported on the capture of Manila. Coverage of the conflict was often sensationalized as Hearst and Pulitzer avidly competed for readers.*

Hearst snaps a photograph of a wrecked Spanish warship from a vessel off Santiago at the onset of the Spanish-American War.

the *Journal* on its special enterprise, and to express the hope that it indicates similar modification of methods and standards in other departments.[38]

Hearst was more than pleased with the current state of his paper's "methods and strategies." The circulation of both Hearst papers leaped dramatically. Every aspect of the actual conflict, as well as a multitude of "created news" events, were reported in detail during the four-month war, which sometimes led to the publication of forty extras in a single day.[39]

After the war, the *Journal* kept its grip on working-class readers with an editorial platform of pure Progressive politics. Hearst's paper championed such domestic issues as a graduated income tax, direct election of United States Senators, and nationalization of mines, railroads, and telegraph lines, coupled with "destruction of the criminal trusts." Foreign policies were based on the maintenance of a strong navy and the construction of the Panama Canal. All of these issues were popular with the working-class men and women whom Hearst courted as regular readers.[40]

Hearst was no longer the callow Western newcomer. His papers were successful, his reputation for boldness recognized. The Democratic party not only hailed Hearst as an ally, but now sought his direct support as well. In the spring before the 1900 elections

I think the standing of the paper will profit by my being here. Other proprietors are safely at home—and I will be soon.[37]

Hearst returned to New York unharmed, his exploits the subject of an editorial both congratulatory and chiding in the New York *Times*:

> The editor and proprietor of the *Journal* of this city showed more than usually good judgment when he assigned Mr. W.R. Hearst to duty as a staff correspondent…. The copy [he] turned out is notably superior…. We venture to congratulate

he conferred with party leaders, who suggested very pointedly that there was no successful Democratic paper in Chicago. Hearst was already contemplating Chicago as the home of his third paper, but he believed that the paper must be started from scratch and must be on the stands in six weeks to be influential in the coming election. One veteran journalist noted:

> No one but W.R. Hearst with… his refusal to recognize the impossible, would have even considered starting a great metropolitan daily newspaper from scratch in six weeks at the turn of the century. Even in those days such a venture would ordinarily take months and possibly a year or more. Today it would be preceded by a couple of years of market surveys and months of advertising campaigns.[41]

Nevertheless, Hearst proceeded. First he sent his longtime business manager, Solomon Carvalho, and his most able editor, Arthur Brisbane, on to Chicago in advance. He gathered a group of reporters and editors to travel with him to Chicago, along with a cargo of new presses shipped from New York. Contracts were made for staff and supplies. He persuaded Democratic presidential candidate William Jennings Bryan to push the button that started the presses for the first time. On July 4, 1900, the first edition of the *Chicago American* was distributed.

In late October, Hearst made his public debut as a political force, appearing at a rally in Madison Square Garden.

HARPER'S WEEKLY

AMERICAN EDITORS. IV.—W. R. HEARST

Puck

Hearst made no speech, being responsible only for calling the throng to order and introducing the party chair. He appeared to enjoy his brief appearance in the political spotlight very well, "laughing outright when some individual in the crowd yelled, 'Three cheers for Willie Hearst!' "[42]

No matter how enthusiastic the crowds, he held no hopes for the election of Bryan and was proved correct in November. Undaunted, Hearst continued his close alliance with the leaders behind the scenes in the Democratic party. Based on the initial success of the Chicago paper, he also found time to start a morning edition.

But his thoughts were not devoted exclusively to papers and politics. After forty years of bachelorhood, William Randolph Hearst had decided to marry. His bride, a New York City dancer, was Millicent Veronica Willson.

The success of Hearst's New York and Chicago papers and his support of Democratic presidential nominee Willam Jennings Bryan drew national attention.

CHAPTER THREE

The Hearst Empire

Phoebe Apperson Hearst was not pleased about her son's impending marriage. She had hoped that he would form an alliance with a woman from a prominent, well-born family. Will had had one serious romance with a San Franciscan named Eleanor Calhoun during his years at Harvard. While Miss Calhoun's family was impeccable, descending from John C. Calhoun, statesman and senator from South Carolina, the young woman— a protégé of Phoebe's—desired a Shakespearean stage career. An actress as daughter-in-law was completely unacceptable to Phoebe. When George Hearst joined his wife in opposing the match, the relationship withered and eventually died.

Phoebe was predictably even less pleased when, in 1902, Hearst married twenty-one-year-old Millicent Willson, a Brooklyn-born chorus girl and daughter of vaudevillians. Millicent first met Hearst in the autumn of 1896, when she appeared with her sister, Anita, eight times a week at the Herald Square Theater in a musical called *The Girl from Paris*. Millicent later recalled her first post-show outing with Hearst, made in the company of her sister:

> Well, he took us down to the *Journal*—the New York *Journal*— we'd hardly heard of it, and he showed us over it, all over it. I hadn't the foggiest notion of what we were doing, walking miles on rough boards in thin, high-heeled evening slippers, and I thought my feet would kill me.

W. R. Hearst posed in a hotel room during a serious moment on the campaign trail. He held office as a congressman from New York for two terms (1902–1906), and ran—unsuccessfully— for mayor of New York City (1904), governor of New York (1906), and president of the United States (1908 and 1912).

Millicent Veronica Willson
(1882–1974)

Of course, this wasn't our idea of a good time. We wanted to go to Sherry's or Bustanoby's. More than that Anita kept whispering to me, "We're going to get thrown out of here, Milly, the way he behaves you'd think he owned it."[1]

The sisters Willson were soon fixtures on Will's nightly perambulations about town, much to the dismay of Phoebe and her accountant, Edward Hardy Clark, whom she dispatched to Manhattan with the thankless task of keeping an eye on the young publisher. "The sight of Will Hearst, with a young girl on either arm, promenading through the streets, snuggled together in a hansom cab, or touring the *Journal* offices was quite scandalous, even for New York,"[2] notes Hearst biographer David Nasaw.

In the opinion of muck-racking journalist Upton Sinclair, Hearst took great pleasure in defying all conventions of polite society:

> One young society man who had known Hearst well spoke with real gravity: "It wasn't what he did—we all do it: but it was the way he did it. He didn't take the trouble to hide what he did."[3]

Late in 1899, Hearst invited the two young women and their parents on an extended holiday abroad. For Hearst, they were a fresh audience to which the sights of Europe could be enthusiastically presented. He never tired of overseas holidays, but preferred to bring a group of fellow travelers who could be depended upon to share his enthusiasm for cathedrals, art galleries and other Hearstian delights.

Will and Millicent's wedding was a small affair, attended by approximately thirty guests. Childhood friend and artist Orrin Peck served as Will's best man; Anita Willson was maid of honor for her sister. The service was held in Grace Episcopal Church in New York City on April 28, 1903, the day before Hearst's fortieth birthday. Both the official betrothal and wedding announcements omitted the bride's theatrical background. Pleading illness, Phoebe Hearst did not attend the ceremony and refused Will's invitation to join them in Europe on their honeymoon.

On that trip, the newlyweds bought an automobile, still a rarity, and traveled through northern Italy. A later stop in London brought Hearst's attention back to business. He had been pondering the wisdom of entering the national magazine market, which was booming the way newspapers had when he began his publishing career sixteen years before. The British magazine, *The Car*, inspired him to begin a similar automobile magazine, which he christened *Motor*. The magazine was so successful it spawned a second Hearst publication, *Motor Boating*. Other magazine titles were added to the Hearst stable, including *Popular Mechanics, Harper's Bazaar* (purchased for the bargain price of $10,000) and *Good Housekeeping*. By the mid-1930s, nine Hearst magazines reached more than twelve million American readers. An English division of the magazine company was created, which published *Connoisseur* and *Nash's* as well as British editions of *Good Housekeeping* and *Harper's Bazaar*. The Hearst International Magazine Corporation was formed in 1905 when Hearst purchased *Cosmopolitan* magazine, which featured weighty, thought-provoking articles by such distinguished contributors as Winston Churchill, Albert Einstein, H.G. Wells and George Bernard Shaw.

When Will and Millicent returned from their wedding journey, they traveled to the family's Babicora ranch in Chihuahua, and then on to Mexico City, where they were received by the country's president, Porfirio Díaz. They next journeyed to Phoebe Hearst's hacienda outside Pleasanton, California. Although there is no record of Millicent's first meeting with the formidable Phoebe Apperson Hearst, Millicent was determined to prove herself a worthy wife and daughter-in-law. She gave up her career on the stage shortly after meeting Hearst. Once wed, she dedicated her life to husband and children, genteel society, and philanthropy, just as Phoebe had forty years earlier.

The couple returned to Manhattan to the four-story house on Lexington

Millicent Willson Hearst at the time of her marriage.

Avenue Hearst had purchased the year before. Martin Dunn, who worked on the night desk at the *Journal*, remembered that Will and Millicent would regularly come into the office after a night on the town. He would work for hours, while Millicent often slept curled up in a chair. Biographer Swanberg reports

> domesticity brought few changes to Hearst. He still got to bed in the neighborhood of 3 and rose sometime before noon. Proud of his lovely young wife, he took her to so many Broadway first nights that she eventually tired of them. He never did.[4]

Millicent's bond with her mother-in-law strengthened and she corresponded faithfully with Phoebe,

Phoebe Apperson Hearst poses with her second grandchild, William Randolph Hearst, Jr., at her country house near Pleasanton, California.

his mother, making frequent trips with his family to visit Phoebe's Pleasanton estate. Shortly after George's birth, Hearst proposed a visit to Phoebe, writing,

> I want [the baby] to know his grandma. He knows the picture and kisses that, and it can't be very satisfactory just to lick the varnish off photographs. I think he would prefer the real article, and I think you would prefer the real baby.[6]

As Hearst's business and political trips occupied more of his time, Millicent and the children began to stay at the Hacienda for extended periods, benefiting from the sunshine, country air, and Phoebe Hearst's attention.

On April 18, 1906, San Francisco was struck early in the morning by a massive earthquake along the San Andreas Fault. At least 664 people died in the quake itself, 28,000 buildings were destroyed, and 200,000 residents were left homeless in the aftermath of the temblor and the fires that burned for days afterward. Millicent was staying at the Pleasanton ranch with her first son, while Phoebe visited Paris and Will tended to business in New York City. She wrote to Phoebe of the disaster:

> We are very happy here at the Hacienda except for the dreadful calamity the people round about us have suffered. The Hacienda escaped without much damage. Nothing inside was broken, except one vase and a few plates in the china closet,

reporting news of her perennially busy husband and her growing family. Their first child, George Randolph, was born in New York City on April 10, 1904. The birth of her first grandson, who was named for her husband, thawed Phoebe somewhat. Four more children, all boys, would follow: William Randolph, Jr., in 1908, John Randolph in 1909, and twins Elbert Willson[5] and Randolph Apperson, in 1915.

The letters from both Will and Millicent during the early years of their marriage reflect a happy, prosperous family. Although the Hearsts lived in Manhattan and Phoebe had returned to California after selling her Washington residence, Will remained close to but the chimneys were all thrown down and the fireplace in Will's room at the top of the house was wrecked.… San Francisco is a dreadful sight. There is nothing left of it but heaps of burnt bricks and piles of twisted iron. Railroad tracks are laid through the middle of the town and construction trains are carrying off the debris just as if they were grading for a new road. Still the people are beginning to revive. Little one story frame houses like in the mining camp are being put up and in these shacks are located some of the biggest firms of the city.…

Will is losing forty thousand dollars a month income from the *Examiner* but thinks the paper will be making money again soon. Our papers have done a great deal of good. They raised about a quarter of a million dollars for the sufferers and established relief camps and hospitals and supply stations…

Our big hospital was taken over by the government, but we are still maintaining a maternity hospital. There are twenty-four women in it and five babies have been born. One is named Phoebe Hearst something and another was named Millicent Hearst something but there was no William Hearst as no boy babies have come along yet.[7]

When the night editor of the New York *American* (formerly the *Journal*) awakened Hearst at his Lexington Avenue apartment with the first news of the earthquake, he unaccountably dismissed its news value by explaining

to the excited editor that earthquakes were commonplace in California. Hearst then wrote a boosterish editorial for the New York paper stating,

Californians don't wholly approve of earthquakes, but they prefer them to cyclones or tornadoes or floods or protracted heat or lightning storms. All of the earthquakes that have occurred in California since it was discovered nearly four hundred years ago have not killed so many people as one or two great cyclones of the Middle West.[8]

Once Hearst realized the extent of the temblor's damage, he drew on all the resources at his disposal. His Chicago, New York, and Los Angeles newspapers sent

Above: Millicent Hearst and her three eldest sons pose with their grandmother.
Below: In a rare show of cooperation, Hearst's Examiner *and two other San Francisco papers issued a joint edition in the wake of the 1906 earthquake and fire.*

W. R. and Millicent Hearst, on the evening they hosted a costume party as a house-warming for their new flat on Riverside Drive in Manhattan.

seventeen well-publicized relief trains carrying medical personnel, food, clothing, and hospital supplies. He sent telegraphic orders to Oakland directing the efforts to get the *Examiner* on the streets again as he left for the stricken city, bearing nearly $200,000 that had been raised by continuing newspaper drives. Upon reaching San Francisco, he saw the rubble that remained as the only sign of his hard-won *Examiner* building. No consolation was drawn from the fact that the *Chronicle* and *Call* were also burned out of their buildings.

Once the immediate crisis had passed, Hearst took his family on a trip to the San Simeon ranch. He derived great satisfaction from continuing the tradition of family visits to San Simeon, though Hearst's notions of camping were vastly more luxurious than his childhood trips with his father. Instead of the blankets on the ground George Hearst had favored, Will, Millicent, their children, and the domestic help retired at night to elaborate canvas tents, pitched upon wooden flooring, and partitioned into four rooms. Separate tents were erected for dining, sleeping, and storage, grouped around "a great circus tent with board flooring covered with soft, warm rugs rich as those of a Bedouin chieftain's."[9] Erecting Hearst's tent

village was a laborious matter, for he favored a site at the ranch that came to be known as Camp Hill, some five miles inland and nearly 1,600 feet above sea level.

While at San Simeon, Hearst "amused himself by writing, directing and photographing cinema plays, using members of the family, guests, even…pets as actors, and showing pictures in the Big Top every night to the squealing glee of the youngsters."[10] Of their first visit to the ranch after the San Francisco earthquake, Millicent wrote to Phoebe:

> We have been down the coast as far as Paso Robles and from there to the ranch where we had a very delightful time. I don't think any place in California has suited the baby as well as the ranch. He played on the beach every day and got sunburned and as strong and healthy as a little indian. We also enjoyed ourselves. We camped out [near] the Burnett [peak] and on the hill tops. We were there two weeks and enjoyed every moment of the time....
>
> We are going up to Mendocino County to see the red woods. Then we are coming back and will have to go East. We hate to leave California. The Hacienda is so beautiful and the crysanthemums will soon be in bloom. We dread going back to the hot red brick houses and the dusty streets of New York.[11]

However reluctant the Hearst

family was to return to the East Coast, it was necessary because of William Randolph Hearst's growing political influence. In 1902, the Democratic Party, in recognition of his support during the William Jennings Bryan presidential campaign two years before, secured Hearst's nomination to the House of Representatives from a West Side district of Manhattan. Hearst would win re-election two years later from the same district.[12]

Hearst prided himself on his individualism and his influence, but these traits did not work to his advantage as a freshman Congressional representative. His Democratic colleagues were chary of Hearst's strong and straightforward endorsement of liberal Progressive issues, from public ownership of utilities to the eight-hour workday. His unwillingness to compromise on such issues further eroded his "infinitesimal support in the first session of the 58th Congress," resulting in the death in committee of every bill he submitted.[13] He secured an appointment to the House Labor Committee through his union connections, which further alienated his colleagues who were dependent upon the traditional method of working through the House party leader, John Sharp Williams. Hearst's most effective work in the House was accomplished on this committee, through his organization of a "small group of radical Democrats, who did his floor work

and followed his lead on committees. In Hearst's own committee appearances, he surprised reporters with his presentation and command of the issues."[14]

Before he began his second term in Congress, Hearst made a concerted bid for the office of mayor of New York City. Despite the high pitch and softness of his voice, Hearst had developed into an effective stump speaker, wooing the working-class vote from the podium as well as the editorial pages. The non-Hearst New York papers did not endorse him; the *Times* viewed the successful tide of his candidacy with alarm. In one of several attempts to discredit him, the *Times* noted his large support among lower East Side neighborhoods, where Hearst's carriage was stopped one day by this chant from his supporters:

> Hoist, Hoist,
> He is not the woist;
> We are for Hoist,
> Last and foist.[15]

The consensus among contemporary observers and political historians is that Hearst won this closely contested race against incumbent George

Top: A 1911 issue of Puck lampooned Hearst's populist campaigns for political office. Above: Ads for Hearst's New York mayoral campaign appeared in his own papers.

"Money Talks," proclaims the cover of this 1906 Puck *magazine skewering Hearst.*

McClellan, but Tammany, the political machine that controlled New York, rigged the election to return their incumbent to office. The final count revealed that Hearst had drawn 38.1 percent of the vote, while McClellan polled 38.7 percent, or a difference of only 3,000 votes out of a total of 600,000 cast.

Hearst returned to Congress, but he had lost what little interest he displayed in the legislative process. His appearances on the floor and in committee were few; his small coalition of radical Progressives had unraveled. Hearst's eye was now on the greatest political prize: the Presidency of the United States of America.

As his last term in Congress drew to a close, Hearst found himself at the zenith of his political power. He owned the strongest Democratic papers in San Francisco, New York, Chicago, Los Angeles, and Boston, whose combined circulation reached two million readers per day.

A competing paper, the New York *Evening Post*, called Hearst "…a low voluptuary trying to sting his senses to a fresh thrill by turning from private to public corruption" and labeled his campaign "a new horror in American politics."[16] A series of articles in *Collier's* magazine, unflattering to Hearst, acknowledged his growing political power and influence. Hearst, William Jennings Bryan, and Theodore Roosevelt were named the country's three major politicians by the Baltimore *Sun*, a non-Hearst paper.[17]

Hearst won the Democratic Party nomination for governor of New York in 1906, an office he considered a stepping-stone to the White House. Conservative party officials were upset by the nomination, but their dissatisfaction grew when—in a remarkable turnabout—Hearst now courted the crooked Tammany machine. Although his campaign reiterated Hearst's endorsement of labor unions, public ownership of utilities, and trust-busting, his support from radical Progressives virtually disappeared after he approached Tammany. The Democratic Party leaders in New York opposed his candidacy, resentful of his journalistic power and suspicious of his independent methods. At Theodore Roosevelt's behest, the Republican Party overlooked their incumbent and nominated Charles Evans Hughes, who had a strong trust-busting record. Hearst persevered in his campaign despite the forces arrayed against him. At a huge rally in Madison Square Garden the night before the election, Hearst called for greater regulation of big business, stating "one law-defying millionaire in jail" would provide the impetus.[18]

Hearst once again lost by an amazingly close margin. Hughes defeated him by 60,000 votes out of 1.5 million cast. This loss effectively ended both his political career and his

Presidential chances. Although he had publicly ended his political career, Hearst decided to run for president in the 1908 elections as an independent.

His wife was concerned about the amount of pressure her husband was under from his business and political interests. Millicent wrote to Phoebe in October of 1907:

> We have been having a very lively time here. There has been a campaign on and a [financial] panic and Will has been in both. One night Will was trying to learn his speech in time to go to six meetings while [Hearst accountant] Edward Clark was explaining how everything was going to pieces in Wall Street and we would all be broke in the morning. Will went out without his dinner and wouldn't eat anything when he came back and I thought that was too much and made him stop speaking for a few days….Will thinks the situation has cleared somewhat but he never leaves the telephone until after banking hours.
>
> We have been neglecting our flat on account of our other troubles but your nice letter and the offer of the tapestries got us interested in the flat again and we went up there today to see where we could put such lovely things….[19]

The flat Millicent mentioned in this letter actually consisted of the top three floors of the posh Clarendon apartment building at 137 Riverside Drive. Hearst's habitual acquisition of antiquities and works of art, as well as

the birth of their second child, made the move from Lexington Avenue imperative. The newest of the Hearst residences was enormous, encompassing over 33,000 square feet, although it soon was filled to capacity with Hearst's latest purchases from the auction houses and art galleries.

Hearst tried again in 1912 to win the presidency as an independent, but his efforts were doomed. His public political career would be limited to two terms in the House, but he remained a powerful figure behind the scenes, courted by Democratic candidates not only for public endorsement in his newspapers, but also for his private affirmation to other party leaders. Although Hearst no longer made news as a politician, his publishing empire made him a political power broker.

As Hearst once again concentrated on the production and distribution of news, he considered the potential of motion pictures to report the news. Initially, audiences were captivated by filmed versions of such commonplace events as London churchgoers walking through Hyde Park in 1889. As the sophistication of these audiences grew, everyday events were no longer a novelty on film. The producers of "actualities," as the first newsreels were called, found that major news events could be enhanced or even recreated in studios using special

Hearst campaigning for governor of New York in 1906.

This trade ad promised theater owners who subscribed to Hearst's first newsreel production "big events...throbbing with live news interest in every foot of film."

effects. Turn-of-the century audiences were then treated to a glimpse of such events as the funeral of Queen Victoria and the subsequent coronation of Edward VII, the devastation of the San Francisco earthquake and fire, and the christening of the *Titanic*. By 1909 the popularity of these topical films led one writer to theorize, "It is quite possible to give each day a few items of the news of a great city by means of moving pictures, and if regularly practiced and advertised it should be not only a feasible scheme but one promising profits."[20]

William Randolph Hearst entered the newsreel business in 1913 at the urging of Edgar Hatrick, the Hearst executive in charge of photographic services. Though Hatrick had counseled Hearst to begin a newsreel as early as 1911, the first news event filmed for a Hearst production was Woodrow Wilson's inauguration early in 1913. From this modest beginning, Hearst newsreels flourished into the mid-1950s and continued to be shown in theaters until 1967.

When Hearst entered the field, the front-runners in the field of motion picture news were Vitagraph, Pathé Freres, and Biograph. Hearst quickly joined forces with a newsreel pioneer, Colonel William Selig, who had first combined journalism with motion pictures in 1903. *The Hearst-Selig News Pictorial* made its debut on February 28, 1914. Trade advertising for this premiere promised:

> Every week in the year...the big events of the whole world will be caught in the happening by Selig moving picture cameras, operated by the trained news gatherers of Hearst's great International News Service which covers the entire globe, and these news pictures, throbbing with live news interest in every foot of film, will be released to you weekly.[21]

In the turbulent early years of the motion picture business, production companies were born, married, divorced, or died with lightning speed. Hearst's newsreel companies were no exception to this rule. Though successful, the Hearst-Selig partnership was short-lived. By January, 1916, Hearst had combined forces with Vitagraph, producing *The Hearst-Vitagraph Weekly Series*. In six months, this partnership had folded and Hearst's company released its own films for the remainder of the year under the title *The International Weekly*.

At the beginning of 1917, Hearst joined forces with another former rival, Pathé, but this alliance only lasted one year. From 1918 until 1920, Hearst remained independent, producing *The International Newsreel*. The Hearst name was conspicuously absent from this latest venture, leading his rivals to speculate that Hearst's opposition to American intervention in World War I had cost him viewers.[22]

By 1918, four newsreel companies had survived the fluctuations of the early years: Hearst, Pathé, Universal and Fox. These four, together with Paramount's 1927 entry, would control how American viewers perceived major events for the next three decades.[23]

Because he was the only major newspaper publisher to enter the field, Hearst's preference for news combined with entertainment had a major influence on the organization and presentation of newsreels. As the medium matured, it followed the format and the style of current newspapers, emphasizing the most sensational events for lead stories, using large, easily understood headlines, and providing specialized features on homemaking and sporting events.[24]

As motion pictures grew in popularity, the major movie studios were eager to form alliances with the established newsreel companies. The affiliation between a movie studio and a newsreel company was mutually beneficial, providing the journalists with operating capital and the studio with current events footage for the programs that changed biweekly at studio-run theatres.

Between 1927 and 1929, Hearst produced separate newsreels for two studios, Universal and Metro-Goldwyn-Mayer. In 1929, as part of the Cosmopolitan Productions contract he made with MGM, Hearst agreed to produce two newsreels exclusively for that studio. At the end of July, 1929, a silent called *The MGM International Newsreel* made its premiere. Its production was targeted for smaller, rural theatres that had not yet installed sound equipment. The second newsreel was a sound production entitled *Hearst Metrotone News*, which became the staple at MGM's growing number of theatres.

By 1915, Hearst was interested in the possibilities motion pictures offered outside the realm of journalism and news. Hearst's uncanny timing, perhaps inherited from his prospector father, brought him to moviemaking at an early point. Of the early years of filmmaking, historian Terry Ramsaye observed, "Trouble and the motion picture business became synonymous. There was safety and assurance nowhere for anyone engaged in the affairs of the screen—but there was always ahead the vision of vast profits."[25]

Hearst's financial risk at the beginning was relatively low, for his first ventures in the nascent picture industry were linked to his successful chain of newspapers. In 1913 the *Chicago Tribune*, feeling pressured by Hearst's *American*, published a newspaper serial story called *The Adventures of Kathlyn*. The twist came when the *Tribune* announced that its readers could also see the serial in the theatres.

A bevy of MGM starlets posed on a sound truck to promote Hearst's new "talking" Metrotone newsreels.

Sheet music promoted Hearst's popular Perils of Pauline *serial. The lyrics poked fun at the implausible plots: "One night she's drifting out to sea/Then they tie her to a tree/I wonder what the end will be/poor Pauline."*

Biweekly episodes were produced by the Chicago-based Selig Polyscope Company. The *Tribune* reported a remarkable ten percent increase in circulation, which sent competitors scrambling for their own newspaper/film combinations.

Hearst, in his inimitable style, immediately adopted the idea and expanded upon it. He contracted with Pathé to produce *The Perils of Pauline*. As the episodes were released, Hearst simultaneously ran the serial in all of his newspapers. An advertising campaign further promoted the parallel venture, calling *Pauline* the "novel you can see in stirring MOTION PICTURES." On March 23, 1914, the premiere of the serial's film version, starring twenty-five-year-old actress Pearl White, took place at Loew's Broadway Theater.[26] It was an instant success in theaters, proving the trade-advertising slogan, "Pauline Pulls People."[27]

Not only did Hearst attend the premiere of his latest venture, but he is also said to have contributed to the plot of *Pauline*, which is remembered today as a classic of the early silent motion picture serials. An orphaned young woman, Pauline Marvin, seeks her lost inheritance with the aid of her stepbrother, Harry, who secretly loves her. A villain named Koerner, whom Pauline never suspects, covets her fortune and hopes to purloin it from her, without revealing his own duplicity. Pauline depends upon her own

luck and pluck (and some last minute intervention by the faithful Harry) to see her through hair-raising encounters with sailors, gypsies, cowboys, pirates, and other henchmen the villain spurs into action. Remarkably, each biweekly episode was complete in itself and did not rely upon a cliff-hanger ending, as had *The Adventures of Kathlyn*.

If Hearst needed additional evidence of the serial's popularity, it was demonstrated the day White was unintentionally set adrift in a balloon. A strong wind and a loosely tied rope sent the actress aloft over New York City during the filming of a scene. Showing as much pluck as her character, White controlled her descent to a vacant lot by letting gas out of the balloon. The actress recalled:

> There seemed to be a million faces looking up at me as that basket finally picked out a spot to settle down on, and then it was caught by eager hands....Word went up from the back of the crowd that I was Pauline of "The Perils" and those in the back crowded forward and those forward had to push to hold their places.... One man snatched my purse for a souvenir, so he said. Another man told him to return it and hit him when he refused. The friends of the first man came to his help and about ten fights ensued. Another man took out his penknife and cut a big piece of my coat; this, also, for a souvenir. Others saw him and did

the same thing…. If it hadn't been for the mounted police coming to my rescue, that would have been my last peril….[28]

While the *Kathlyn* serial had boosted circulation for the *Tribune*, *The Perils of Pauline* did not do the same for the Hearst papers. As one early cinema historian theorized, "The conservative *Tribune* used the motion picture to reach into the emotion-hungry nickelodeon audiences. The vivid Hearst newspapers, Brisbaned and comic-stripped, already had that class of following and the motion picture could add nothing to their pulling power."[29]

The success of the film version was more than enough for Hearst. His company and Pathé began work immediately on a follow-up series designed to capitalize on Pauline's momentum. *The Exploits of Elaine*, a 1915 production—again featuring Pearl White—was also short on plot but compensated with an abundance of action. Elaine searched through each episode for her father's murderer, encountering the first of the silent screen's unseen menaces, the Clutching Hand. Truly a terrible figure, the Clutching Hand had stooped shoulders, a turned-up collar, and a face that was never visible. Elaine Dodge was described in the newspaper serial as

both the ingenue and the athlete— the thoroughly modern type of

girl—equally at home with tennis and tango, table talk and tea. Vivacious eyes that hinted at a stunning amber brown sparkled beneath masses of the most wonderful auburn hair. Her pearly teeth, when she smiled, were marvelous. And she smiled often, for life to her seemed a continuous film of enjoyment.[30]

Needless to say, Elaine was more than equal to the Clutching Hand's nefarious schemes, which included poisoned wallpaper. ("That wall paper has been loaded down with arsenic! I thought I knew the smell the moment I got a whiff of it. This Clutching Hand is a diabolical genius!")

Another Hearst-Pathé production in 1916 was *Beatrice Fairfax*, starring Grace Darling. The name of this newest serial heroine was chosen for its recognition value. For the past fifteen years, Hearst had run an advice-to-the-lovelorn column in his papers. The advice was dispensed by a Hearst staff member, Marie Manning, who used Beatrice Fairfax as her pen name. The column proved so popular that it was advertised with this jingle:

Just write to Beatrice Fairfax
Whenever you're in doubt;
Just write to Beatrice Fairfax
And she will help you out.[31]

The serial version of Beatrice Fairfax ran in a "photostrip" in the daily papers. Frames from the film were reproduced along with the

A WORD *to the* EXHIBITORS *of* AMERICA

"The plain facts seem to justify *the* assertion that Cosmopolitan Productions have scored more successful pictures than any other producing organization in the moving picture business because-"

by WILLIAM RANDOLPH HEARST

One year after Hearst formed Cosmpolitan Productions, he released this 1920 advertisement to movie theater owners, celebrating the release of seven pictures and promising "sincere and unceasing effort" to produce the "best in every phase of motion picture making" in the future.

narrative, which further popularized the serial as visual entertainment.

The last of the great Hearst-Pathé serial films was the 1917 production of *Patria*, starring Irene Castle. The dancing partner of Vernon Castle, Irene was billed as "the best known woman in America today." The phenomenal success of the husband-and-wife dancing team led to the popularity of ballroom dancing and the proliferation of clothing, candy, cosmetics, nightclubs, hairstyles, shoes, tooth powder, and other products and services endorsed by one or both Castles. While her husband served with the Royal Air Force in World War I, Irene Castle signed a contract with Hearst-Pathé and began filming at their Fort Lee, New Jersey, studios. She described the plot of *Patria* as

> …a little jewel. I was Patria Channing, the sole heir to one hundred million dollars I didn't know about and the sole survivor of the "Fighting Channings," a family of munitions-makers dedicated to American Freedom. Warner Oland [later to play Charlie

Chan] played the grimacing Baron Huroki, who schemed to have me replaced by a villainess named Elaine (who by coincidence was my exact double) who would put my little bundle of a hundred million dollars at the disposal of him and his Mexican confederates.[32]

Hearst footed the $90,000 bill for the production of *Patria*, which had fifteen episodes. Although Patria finally rescued the United States almost single-handedly, the film was meant to be a warning to American citizens to exercise vigilance against Japan and Mexico. (Hearst's unfavorable opinion of Mexico was probably formed during the period just before *Patria* was filmed, when Pancho Villa and his compatriots were responsible for a number of depredations at the Hearst family's huge Mexican ranches.) The film was banned in some parts of the country because it was considered too extreme. President Woodrow Wilson asked Hearst to have the virulent anti-Japanese scenes edited. Hearst complied, but the film failed at the box office.

By 1917, Hearst decided to branch out on his own to begin production of feature-length motion pictures. Entertainment, always the keystone of his journalistic philosophy, was now the focus of his newest company. Initially named International Films, the company became Cosmopolitan Productions at the end of the decade. Hearst's first Cosmopolitan motion picture studio was located in a mammoth brick building that covered an entire city block in Manhattan between Second Avenue and 125th Street. Once a popular German *beirgarten* called Sulzer's Harlem River Park Casino had flourished on the site. When Prohibition caused the business to close, Hearst renovated the property, filling it with expensive camera equipment and a sizeable staff.[33]

Hearst moved into the picture business the same way he had conquered publishing: he offered high salaries to attract talented workers who were supplied with ample operating budgets. The first actress he signed was Alma Rubens, a twenty-year-old native of San Francisco whose true name was Alma Smith. Famed for her classical beauty, Rubens appeared in D.W. Griffith's 1916 epic, *Intolerance*.

Hearst employed other assets at his command. His magazines provided stories that experienced writers turned into screenplays, his theater and film connections yielded experienced actors and technicians, and his network of newspapers provided ample publicity.

One of the few historians to consider Hearst's place in cinema history wrote,

> [Hearst] was one of the first to use Technicolor, to do a musical, to insist upon historical accuracy (even though it was not an ethic of his newspaper publishing), but he

is seldom cited in film histories for any of this…. If Hearst had given his filmmaking the same enormous energy and obsessive preoccupation he gave his newspapers, his movies might have been successful enough to accord him a place in film history at least on a level with [British producer] Alexander Korda, a man who had similar tastes in subject matter…." [34]

In December of 1917, he attended a special screening of *Runaway, Romany*, a film produced by friend and fellow newspaper publisher, Paul Bloch. The film starred Marion Davies, a veteran of stage musical comedies, who was about to turn twenty-one. Hearst and Davies first met two years before, when she was appearing in the Irving Berlin revue *Stop! Look! Listen!* Although Bloch was pessimistic about the probable success of *Runaway*—which was his first venture in film-making, as well as Davies' cinematic debut—Hearst saw a wealth of possibilities that could be improved upon in the next film Davies made. At the end of the screening, Hearst realized two things: he wanted to produce Davies' next picture and he was very taken with her.

Marion Davies was born Marion Cecelia Douras in Brooklyn on January 3, 1897. A stunning blue-eyed blonde, she made her Broadway debut in 1911 in Charles Dillingham's production of *The Lady and the Slipper*. Davies biographer Fred Lawrence

The Love Piker, *an early production of Hearst's Cosmopolitan Productions, premiered on July 22, 1923 and featured Anita Stewart, a star under contract to Hearst.*

Top: Marion Davies graced a 1920 cover of Theatre Magazine *at the age of 23. Above: In 1920, Davies also starred in* April Folly, *her seventh film for Hearst.*

Guiles describes her during this period as

> a new kind of young woman, soon to be emancipated from more than her bustle. She radiated vitality and wholesome good cheer along with a latent (later realized) flair for parody and comedy that would keep her working for the next twenty-two years.... To nearly everyone who met her, she seemed as effervescent as champagne and it would seem completely in key with her personality when she developed such a taste for that beverage.[35]

By 1915, Davies was appearing in another Dillingham production entitled *Chin-Chin*. In mid-June she opened in the 1916 edition of Florenz Ziegfeld's *Follies* and parlayed that experience into the Berlin revue, where Hearst first met her backstage. "He sent me flowers and little gifts," Davies recalled in her autobiography, "I wasn't the only one he sent gifts to, but all the girls thought he was particularly looking at me…I think he was a very lonesome man."[36]

Another sign of Hearst's growing affection was the shower of publicity Davies received in the Hearst papers. Hearst became virtually obsessed with the idea of making Davies a star of the first magnitude. He closely supervised screenwriters and directors, ordered *objets d'art* from his vast collections to

dress her movie sets, entertained their industry peers in the film colony at his various estates, and stepped up publicity in his papers. Davies was working overtime: the filming of *Runaway* was sandwiched in between her stage appearances during the summer of 1916. While Hearst searched for a suitable property for her next film, Davies returned to the Broadway stage for three successive 1917 productions: *Oh, Boy, Miss 1917*, and *Words and Music*.

Her first Cosmopolitan production, *Cecilia of the Pink Roses*, premiered in Manhattan on June 3, 1918, with Hearst's flair for showmanship: the picture screen was surrounded with thousands of pink roses, whose fragrance wafted toward the audience by discreetly placed fans. Hearst devised an unprecedented plan to book the film into twelve different theaters in New York City at once.

Hearst's New York *American* declared the film a "masterpiece" and noted "…there were few dry eyes at the Rivoli Theater yesterday when the vision of Marion Davies faded on the screen."[37] The New York *Times*, with more reserve, stated: "There is no objection to Miss Davies. She is by no means a sensational screen actress, but she fills the requirements of her part."[38]

One of Davies' first interviews was published in the October 1919 issue of *Photoplay*. The breathless author relates a personal visit to Davies in her posh new home on Riverside Drive, which Hearst had purchased for her. The interviewer gushed,

> To know that she stuttered, then made her a little less Olympian— the goddess actually moved, talked, laughed and everything... I suspect that her great joy in this home of hers is in manipulating the little lift that carries you from height to superheight—from the salon with the marble fountain on the first to a hall of mirrors, on the second and to a library on the third floor—and I liked her best in the library. It's a long room in old blue—lined with books. Hundreds of books—tiers of them on four walls. Books in rare bindings, first editions, books of history, travel, satire and fiction. "I-I'll read all of these when I'm an old wo-woman," she said and reached up and took down a book.[39]

With Davies' career successfully underway, Hearst struck a deal in mid-1919 with Adolph Zukor's Artcraft and Paramount Pictures Corporation to distribute all of Cosmopolitan's films. The alliance between Hearst and Paramount assured a regular venue for Cosmopolitan Productions throughout the country.

In the midst of his first ventures into feature-length motion picture production, Hearst was called to his mother's deathbed. Ill with influenza since a Christmas visit to her son and his family in New York, Phoebe Hearst had returned to her home in California, but failed to improve. She died there on April 13, 1919, at the age of seventy-six, one of the casualties of the influenza pandemic that claimed more than half a million lives in the United States alone. Once again the San Francisco *Examiner* devoted a black-bordered front page to a death in the Hearst family. Annie Laurie wrote the San Francisco paper's obituary, headlined:

> FRIEND OF ALL,
> NOBLEST OF WOMEN RESTS
> FAREWELL! WISE COUNSELLOR,
> WE STAND UNCOVERED
> AT YOUR PASSING...[40]

Phoebe Apperson Hearst's will provided generous bequests to the University of California at Berkeley and other philanthropic interests that had absorbed her during her 28-year widowhood. Wyntoon, her estate in northern California, was left to her niece, Anne, while her grandsons received the *Examiner* building in San Francisco and the proceeds from the sale of her estate in Pleasanton. But her principal heir was her only child, William Randolph Hearst, who inherited $7.5 million in cash (worth about $87.8 million in 2003 dollars), her stock portfolio, and title to the vast San Simeon ranch.[41]

CHAPTER FOUR

Golden Years at San Simeon

Late one afternoon in April of 1919, William Randolph Hearst and architect Julia Morgan met in her San Francisco office to discuss San Simeon and the prospect of building "something a little different than other people are doing out in California."[1] The coastal ranchland had been in the family for more than 50 years, since the time his father had purchased—often for as little as seventy cents an acre—the original Mexican ranchos of Piedras Blancas, San Simeón, and Santa Rosa.

Shortly before his mother died and he at last gained control of the family fortune, W.R. decided he was "tired of camping out and wanted something more comfortable"[2] on Camp Hill, the location of his family's tent city during summers past. A rocky outcropping 1,600 feet above sea level and five miles inland, the site had sentimental value for Hearst, but presented a series of daunting challenges for his architect. William Randolph Hearst, Jr., the publisher's second son, recalled:

> The experts told Pop that it couldn't be done. No one could build an adequate foundation for a large home up there on the crest of that steep hill overlooking the Pacific and the little village of San Simeon. There was no proper building material available—no lumber, no nearby steel or iron. Even if such materials were [there], a rising, curving road would have to be constructed out of the wilderness. And it was more than a five-mile pull…to the mountaintop…. It was

W. R. Hearst hosted dinners for his San Simeon guests in Casa Grande's Refectory.

Julia Morgan used this student identification card when she studied architecture in Paris at L'École des Beaux-Arts, where she won several medals in competitions.

a crazy idea. The experts told the old man to forget it.[3]

But Julia Morgan *was* an expert and her qualifications made her the ideal choice for the commission. A civil engineer and architect trained in the classical Beaux-Arts tradition, Morgan also had extensive experience working with reinforced concrete in her native California. Her reputation for respecting the wishes of her clients and her diplomatic personality further ensured her success with the demanding Hearst.[4]

Much has been made of the contrast between Hearst's initial request for a "Jappo-Swisso bungalow" and the formidable estate that grew in its place. But that modest structure was abandoned very quickly in favor of a more ambitious plan for a main building (Casa Grande), and guesthouses ("A" House, or Casa del Mar; "B" House, or Casa del Monte, and "C" House, or Casa del Sol), linked by a "plan of walks and flower beds or landscape features…bring[ing] all of the structures together into a harmonious whole."[5] Also added were indoor and outdoor swimming pools, a movie theater with a small stage, tennis courts, a billiard room, wine cellar, two libraries, a private zoo and aviary, dog kennels, landing strip and airplane hangar, Thoroughbred horse

ranch and miles of bridle paths, and a five-mile pergola.

Hearst's wife, Millicent, suggested that the estate be named *Las Estrellas*, but the name was already in use at a neighboring ranch. In its place, Hearst chose the name *La Cuesta Encantada* (The Enchanted Hill). No matter how large his estate grew over the succeeding years, Hearst never referred to it as a "castle." Instead he simply called his hilltop home "the ranch."[6]

Morgan accepted the San Simeon commission virtually at the midpoint of a varied and prolific career. The myth has persisted, however, that Hearst gambled on Morgan's abilities when San Simeon was begun in 1919. In reality, she had been practicing nearly twenty years and had at least 350 other private residences, institutions, churches, estates, and community buildings to her credit at that time. Nine years younger than Hearst, Morgan was raised in Oakland, California. She studied civil engineering at the University of California at Berkeley, where she graduated in 1894. Phoebe Apperson Hearst, a generous benefactor to the university, as well as a strong supporter of education for women, first met Julia Morgan on that campus.

Upon the advice of one of her instructors, architect Bernard Maybeck, Morgan traveled to Paris to study at L'École des Beaux-Arts. When she arrived in 1896, Morgan was refused admission because Beaux-Arts administrators had never even conceived of allowing women to study at the institution. Morgan was eventually admitted in November of 1898 and advanced to the top class within a year. Phoebe Hearst visited the aspiring architect the following year and offered to be her financial sponsor. Although Morgan declined the offer, Mrs. Hearst's gesture encouraged her to persevere. In 1902, she became the first woman to receive Beaux-Arts certification in architecture.

When she returned to San Francisco, Morgan joined the staff of architect John Galen Howard. He had opened an office in Berkeley after winning the competition sponsored by Phoebe Hearst to design and execute a master building plan for the University of California. Under Howard's supervision, Morgan drew the elevations and designed the decorative details for the Mining Building, commissioned by Phoebe Hearst in memory of her mining magnate husband. The Hearst Greek Theater on the Berkeley campus was Morgan's next design under Howard's aegis.

In 1904, she opened her own practice in San Francisco. As Morgan's career developed, she began work on a number of residential commissions in the Piedmont, Claremont, and Berkeley neighborhoods. Morgan was also commissioned by Phoebe Hearst to complete her hacienda near Pleasanton and to complete one of Phoebe's

greatest philanthropic gestures, the seaside retreat for the Young Women's Christian Association called Asilomar.

After her collaboration with W. R. Hearst began, Julia Morgan continued to practice architecture full time from her San Francisco office, devoting her weekends to on-site supervision at San Simeon. As Hearst traveled a great deal, many of their ideas and decisions were committed to paper. Their voluminous correspondence, together with surviving architectural plans, has created a detailed account of San Simeon's construction.

Architectural drafter Warren McClure, who joined Morgan's staff in 1930, was one of several members of her firm who relocated to San Simeon. McClure recalled:

> I was Miss Morgan's man on the job. She did not stay there but made one-day visits every week or so. My little shack office was in the east court and WRH would spend hours in it every day. I recall Miss Davies popping in at times with the question, "What are you kids cooking up now?" The "cooking up" was usually something akin to the Vatican or Windsor Castle to the later disconcerting of Miss Morgan and the treasury. None told him nay, however….[7]

Morgan painstakingly plotted and re-plotted the buildings and grounds to accommodate her client's objectives: undisturbed native oaks, a large main

Top: Architect Julia Morgan in 1926.
Above: Detailed reports via telegrams and letters on construction at San Simeon flowed between Morgan and her most famous client.

Hearst and architect Julia Morgan, photographed by guest and film director Irvin Willat in 1926, review plans on the terrace at his San Simeon estate.

his chronic cash flow problems, he seldom lived up to these terms.

As the San Simeon project grew, Morgan found herself increasingly involved in the operation of the estate as well as its design. Funds from Hearst flowed through her office for the purchase of everything from Spanish antiquities and Hoover vacuum cleaners to Icelandic moss to feed the reindeer in the hilltop zoo. She hired not only the construction and warehouse workers, but the household staff as well.

The massive site's construction workers initially lived in tents, which were later replaced with crude barracks. Morgan had the responsibility not only for hiring laborers, but also for keeping them occupied during their Sundays off. Hearst forbade the workers to "wander over the ranch or to fish or to hunt.... they shall confine themselves to their legitimate business on the property. If you hired a plumber to fix your bathroom you would not expect him to be wandering around your parlor or reading your books in the library...."[9]

Morgan hit upon the idea of showing movies in the remote location. "I have tried a moving picture show once a week...which has been well worth the money in keeping down 'turn-over'. The operator brings his own machine, pays his expenses and shows seven reels for $30.00."[10] The movies were a successful diversion for

terrace and walkways between buildings, splendid views, and superb settings for Hearst's burgeoning collections of art and antiquities. In addition to the estate that exists today, Hearst and Morgan had plans for additional guesthouses and wings for Casa Grande that were never realized.

Early in the project Morgan outlined the fees for her services with Hearst:

> If satisfactory to you, may I suggest that payment for my work be made on this plan: Instead of paying the usual 3½% when the work is begun, and 2½% as it progresses, that your office pay me $500.00 on account on the first of each month until an amount equal to the commission shall have been paid. I have been using this method and have found it satisfactory both to my clients and myself.[8]

Hearst readily agreed, but because of

workers lured by Hearst's high wages, but many were still lonely for families they could not bring to the remote location.

Morgan designed and constructed five different houses in the Mediterranean style for the estate's senior staff and their families. Construction superintendent George Loorz, head gardener Nigel Keep, and maintenance head Marks Harry Eubanks lived in the Spanish-tiled stucco houses on the bay, while Don Pancho Estrada, descendent of the family who held the original Mexican land grants for San Simeon, lived in the house closest to the estate's warehouses. Morgan consulted with each member of the workers' families, including the children, before producing her designs. The fifth house, built nearby in the same Mediterranean vernacular, disguised the estate's poultry ranch. Julia Morgan calculated the cost of constructing the five staff houses at $110,000.

Household staff members were eventually located in an entire wing of Casa Grande. Hearst suggested that Morgan make these rooms large enough "to relieve the discomforts which our best help now experience and which make it difficult to keep them on the Hill."[11]

Hearst lived in "A" House, the first of the guesthouses to be constructed, until Casa Grande was ready for occupancy late in 1925. Never one to

delay gratification, Hearst often invited guests to stay before construction was complete. Severe rainstorms lashed the hilltop during February of 1927, revealing inadequacies in the heating system. After the first storm, Hearst dictated a letter to Morgan, suggesting that the doors to "A" House be made

water and draft proof with metal weather strips. If antique iron doors [do] not permit this, don't use antique iron. Let's have COMFORT AND HEALTH before so much art. The art won't do us any good if we are all dead of pneumonia.[12]

A second storm followed quickly. Greatly put out, he left this note for the construction foreman:

We are all leaving the hill. We are drowned, blown and frozen out. The trouble is not merely with the weather. It is with the houses. …Before we build anything more let's make what we have built practical, comfortable and beautiful. If we can't do that we might just as well change the names of the houses to Pneumonia House, Diphtheria House and Influenza Bungalow. The main house we can call the Clinic. I am not coming back to the hill until we put the small houses on a liveable basis….

W. R. Hearst on the oak-studded hillside below House A (right) and House C, when construction was nearly completed in 1923.

Construction on "Camp Hill" in the early 1920s shows two guesthouses nearing completion and progress on the main building.

…The weather strips wail like a chorus of lost souls, the windows leak little rivers of running water and under the doors the cold droughts blow like…hurricanes until the rugs flop on the floor.

…All who could have left and the few who remain are eagerly waiting a chance to get out.[13]

Despite his threat, Hearst remained on the hilltop. That weekend, he and Morgan considered various methods of weatherproofing the buildings. In April he was still monitoring the progress carefully, stating in one telegram, "WINDOWS NOT WEATHERSTRIPPED…MAKE HOUSES NO BETTER THAN MOVING PICTURE SET…"[14] Hearst's pique eventually subsided along with the winter storms.

In addition to the construction on the seaside hilltop at San Simeon, in the late 1920s Hearst commissioned Morgan to design and build a (relatively) small hacienda near the northern boundaries of his ranch. Located near the tiny settlement of Jolon, the Milpitas Hacienda was built to house cowboys, but also served as an oasis for Hearst and the visitors who accompanied him on strenuous horseback tours of his sprawling ranch. To keep the newspaper mogul in touch with his many enterprises, a telephone line was strung along the thirty-six cowboy camps of the ranch all the way to Jolon, thirty rugged brush-and-rattlesnake-filled miles away from Casa Grande.

Mission San Antonio de Padua is

located less than a mile away from the Milpitas Hacienda. Located on property the Hearsts bought, the Mission had been in a state of disrepair following the secularization of the missions, and completely abandoned after 1882. Phoebe Hearst and her son both contributed to the restoration of the historic structure when the drive to preserve California's twenty-one missions became a popular effort at the turn of the twentieth century. (A great deal of this acreage, including the Milpitas hacienda, was sold to the U.S. Army in the early 1940s.)

The massive construction site at San Simeon inspired this already avid collector to new heights. The flood of Hearst's purchases from Europe became so great that Morgan and her staff members designed an inventory system to work in concert with the International Studio Art Corporation, a new subsidiary of the Hearst Corporation. This operation had a warehouse and offices in New York, where staff members arranged for newly arrived European shipments to be transported either by rail across the country or by ship to ports at San Pedro or San Francisco.

Further arrangements were then made to transport the contents by steamer to San Simeon Bay. In May of 1930, Hearst wrote to Morgan, asking her to buy a moving van to transport his art objects to San Simeon from Los Angeles or San Francisco. Hearst was quite disappointed to find that a van was not immediately available; four weeks would be required to fill the order.[15]

Morgan had reinforced and extended the 1,000-foot pier built by George Hearst in 1878, adding a

An aerial view of Hearst's hilltop San Simeon estate in the late 1920s.

railroad siding so that shipments could be unloaded smoothly and rolled to the series of warehouses she had designed and constructed. Here her staff members photographed and inventoried new shipments, placing them in storage. Eventually some of these architectural elements and art objects were indeed installed in San Simeon or other Hearst estates. Some were sent to Hollywood for use on movie sets or to other cities for loan to museums. Still other shipments were never uncrated. By 1930, the warehouses at San Simeon were full.

Julia Morgan was also retained to work on Wyntoon, another Hearst estate, located on the McCloud River in northern California. A favorite retreat of Phoebe Hearst's, the Wyntoon property was originally the country home of her attorney, Charles W. Wheeler. Enjoying her visits there, Phoebe Hearst ardently wished for an "inexpensive little house" and Wheeler agreed to let her build such a structure on his property for a maximum of $10,000. By the time noted California architect Bernard Maybeck finished his work in 1903, the cost, Phoebe noted, "was much more than I anticipated and reached the total sum of approximately $100,000."[16]

When fire claimed the Maybeck house on the Wyntoon estate in 1929, Hearst retained Morgan to design and construct several chalets on the 50,000–acre forested site. Here Hearst envisioned the perfect setting for some of his first collections, including the German beer steins and Swiss wood-carvings he acquired on his first trip to Europe nearly sixty years earlier. Artist Willy Pogány drew large murals depicting German fairy tales on the exterior walls of the chalets. Morgan's biographer, Sara Holmes Boutelle, noted, "The effect of the 'village' is Bavarian. But the symmetry of each building and the careful siting around the central green are more Beaux-Arts. …Morgan's use of the local stone and wood is characteristically sensitive."[17]

Hearst and Morgan collaborated on several more significant commissions, including an unbuilt hacienda at Babicora, his million-acre ranch in Mexico; the unbuilt "Hopi" residence at the Grand Canyon; and the Phoebe Apperson Hearst Memorial Women's Gymnasium at UC Berkeley. Morgan also supervised the remodeling of Marion Davies' vast beach house in Santa Monica and the unrealized plans to create a wing of the de Young Museum from an entire Spanish monastery Hearst had purchased, dismantled, and ordered shipped to California.

In 1930, Arthur Byne located another monastery for Hearst, the Santa Maria de Ovila, which was erected near Burgos, Spain, sometime before 1213. Byne once again began the laborious process of dismantling and shipping the stones to San Fran-

cisco while Julia Morgan began to draw plans that would incorporate the monastery into the expansion of Wyntoon. A barn-sized structure used by the brothers to store wine was contemplated as a future movie theater. The long and exceedingly narrow main building was once considered for a living room, but existing Morgan plans illustrate its proposed conversion into an indoor swimming pool.

By the time the monastery arrived on eleven ships in San Francisco harbor, Hearst's financial difficulties precluded any of these plans. A fire in the warehouse where the stones were stored obliterated the numbering system, making it impossible to reconstruct the monastery. All that remains of Santa Maria de Ovila is the rubble in San Francisco's Golden Gate Park.

By the mid-1930s, Hearst also had significant real estate holdings in New York City. Hearst and his star editor

Phoebe Apperson Hearst originally left Wyntoon, her northern California estate, to her niece. In 1925, W. R. Hearst purchased it from Anne Apperson Hearst and retained Julia Morgan to design a series of chalets for the estate four years later.

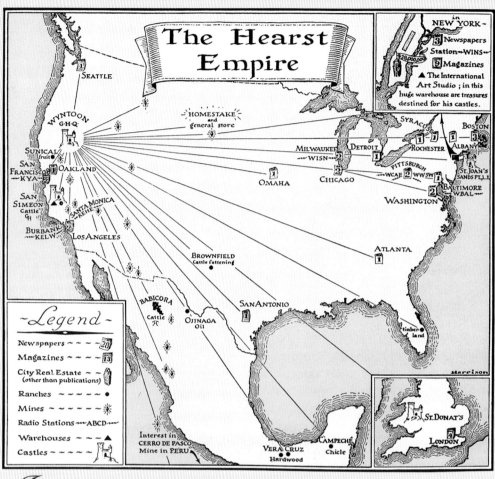

The Hearst Empire

in NEW YORK ~
- ③ Newspapers
- Station ~ WINS
- ⑨ Magazines
- ▲ The International Art Studio ; in this huge warehouse are treasures destined for his castles.

SEATTLE

WYNTOON
G.H.Q.

HOMESTAKE and general store

SUNICAL fruit

SAN FRANCISCO ~ KYA

OAKLAND

SAN SIMEON Cattle GH

SANTA MONICA KEHE

BURBANK ~ KELW

LOS ANGELES

MILWAUKEE ~ WISN ②

DETROIT ①

ROCHESTER

SYRACUSE ①

BOSTON ③

ALBANY

St.JOAN'S SANDS Pt.L.I.

PITTSBURGH ~ WCAE ② WWSW

CHICAGO ②

BALTIMORE WBAL

WASHINGTON

OMAHA ①

ATLANTA ①

BROWNFIELD Cattle fattening

SAN ANTONIO ①

BABICORA Cattle ℛ

OJINAGA Oil

timber land

Interest in CERRO DE PASCO Mine in PERU

VERA CRUZ Hardwood

CAMPECHE Chicle

Harrison

~ Legend ~
- Newspapers ~ ~ ~ 20
- Magazines ~ ~ ~ ~ 13
- City Real Estate ~ ~ (other than publications)
- Ranches ~ ~ ~ ~ ●
- Mines ~ ~ ~ ~ ~ ✸
- Radio Stations ~ ABCD ~
- Warehouses ~ ~ ~ ▲
- Castles ~ ~ ~ ~ 🏰

ST.DONAT'S

LONDON ④

In 1935, Fortune *magazine published an article on Hearst, using this map to illustrate his far-flung business enterprises.*

In 1937, fifty years after he began his career in San Francisco, Hearst publishing ventures reached their apex under W. R.'s direction. Twenty-five daily papers with a combined circulation of over five million readers, and seventeen Sunday papers with nearly six million readers bore the Hearst name. In addition to the direct ownership of newspapers, the Hearst Corporation also owned magazines, radio stations, wire services, syndicates, feature services, paper mills, and distribution centers. Hearst also owned and distributed the *American Weekly,* a Sunday supplement reaching thirty million homes each week.

Today the Hearst Corporation continues to thrive. The company owns twelve daily newspapers and twenty weekly newspapers, eighteen U. S. consumer magazines (including *Town & Country,*

Cosmopolitan, Esquire, and *Good Housekeeping*) with more than a hundred international editions, and a cartoon and features syndication service (King Features). Hearst Business Media publishes electronic databases and business information services in the automotive, electronic, and medical industries.

The Hearst Corporation is also active in cable networks through stakes in A&E, Lifetime, and ESPN. Online services include a stake in the women's Web network iVillage. Through Hearst Argyle Television, they own and manage twenty-eight stations serving more than twenty-four markets around the country. The company also produces syndicated TV programs through a joint venture with NBC, and manages two radio stations in Baltimore. The company is owned by the Hearst family but managed by a board of trustees.

Arthur Brisbane owned twenty-seven acres near Columbus Circle that he planned to develop as the headquarters for the Hearst Corporation, rivaling the newly built Rockefeller Center. But Hearst and Brisbane were caught in the financial cataclysms of the early Depression years and their plans came to nothing. Other Manhattan property owned by Hearst included the Ritz Tower, where he retained a private floor for his New York visits; two other hotels, the Warwick and the Lombardy; Sherwood Studios; and the Ziegfeld and Cosmopolitan theaters. The Hearst Corporation also owned newspaper buildings in eighteen other cities.[18]

Never fond of living in the East, Hearst found little reason to continue to reside in New York with his political dreams in ashes and his marriage cooling. As Hearst returned to San Simeon for increasingly longer periods of time, Millicent Hearst, now a grande dame of café society, divided her time between her Riverside Drive apartment and the former Oliver Hazard Perry Belmont estate at Sands Point, Long Island. Once enthusiastic about California, she seldom traveled to San Simeon after 1925. Instead she fully embraced the high society Hearst had always loathed and raised money for the Free Milk Fund for Babies, a charitable organization she founded in 1921. Their separation was never announced, although W. R. and

W. R. Hearst in Europe in 1934, in search of art and antiques for his collections.

Millicent entered into two legal agreements. The first, signed in 1921, set up a trust fund yielding $10,000 monthly until 1940, when the youngest of their children reached the age of 25. The second agreement, executed in 1927, provided for an additional $10,000 monthly for her support and maintenance and for that of the children when they were with her.[19]

W. R. Hearst's inclination to travel, whether for business or pleasure—coupled with lavish use of telegrams—kept him apprised of his family in the east and his far-flung business ventures. In 1937, fifty years after he began his career in San Francisco, Hearst newspaper enterprises reached their apex. Twenty-five daily papers with a combined circulation of over five million readers, and seventeen Sunday papers with nearly six million readers, bore the Hearst name. In addition to the direct ownership of

his previous decision…. He never said, "Let's talk it over," or "Take it up later." He always gave me definite answers.[20]

With tremendous capacity for detail, Hearst kept abreast of his many publications, assisted by secretary Joseph Willicombe. If any of the army of Hearst employees doubted Hearst's complete control over the editorial policy of his vast number of papers, they soon found that he was in the habit of firing off letters of praise or blame directly to the employee in question. Even though the number of newspapers in his chain had risen dramatically, Hearst had scarcely altered his intensive method of review, described in a 1935 article in *Fortune* magazine:

> On the priceless carpet at his feet there are spread six newspapers worth altogether from twelve to eighteen cents…. The old man— he is seventy-two—is hanging over them with a big black pencil in his hand. Every so often he reaches down and makes a cryptic black mark, with professional ease that smacks of the proof-room. The pencil moves and the marks look as if he were the head copyreader polishing off a final edition amid the rumble of presses under a green lampshade in the small hours of the morning. Though you cannot hear the presses, he can…. He rises now and then, paces along the edge of the newspapers, swooping down

In 1935, W. R. Hearst took a break from a croquet game to make notes on the business log that his personal secretary, Joseph Willicombe (left), compiled daily.

newspapers, the Hearst Corporation also operated wire services, syndicates, feature services, paper mills, and distribution centers.

One of Hearst's newspaper executives, Harry M. Bitner, recalled that he usually traveled to California for a few days each month to confer with the "Chief."

I used to take with me briefcases filled with files on many subjects. Mr. Hearst was never in a hurry to talk after I arrived. He wanted me to rest for a day or two, perhaps to gain a better perspective. Then, during a full afternoon or evening, we would sit down and I would try to summarize, from the files I had brought, each problem or question. When each of my little speeches was ended, he gave his answer, succinct but comprehensive. If I did not always agree, he would listen courteously, analyze my comments, then usually reaffirm when he sees something to correct.... The job is finished. One week's work by an editor a few thousand miles away has been digested, corrected, and stored in that relentless memory.[21]

Hearst brought the same capacity for detail to Cosmopolitan Productions, his feature film company. Although Cosmopolitan films were usually noted for their authentic period furnishings, two Hearst productions designed by Joseph Urban are recognized as the first use of the Art Deco style in films. *Enchantment* (1921) and *The Young Diana* (1922), both starring Marion Davies, were strikingly spare and reflective of the European trend toward the "moderne."[22]

Davies' fifteenth film, the 1922 production of *When Knighthood was in Flower*, was a critical and financial success. Reviewers were enthusiastic about her growth as an actress, the realistic sets (dressed with authentic objects of the period furnished from Hearst's vast and various collections), and the supporting actors, including William Powell playing a black-hearted villain in his first screen performance.

Her success in this elaborate historical epic only reinforced Hearst's conviction that costume drama was the appropriate vehicle for Davies' continuing climb to fame. This assumption of Hearst's unfortunately masked Davies' comedic talents, leaving her stranded

in what critic Pauline Kael has termed "costume clinkers." Hearst's continual emphasis on historical accuracy for props, sets, and costumes drove the budgets of her pictures skyward, making it virtually impossible for the films to turn a profit.

Never shy about publicizing his ventures, Hearst geared up his newspaper chain to ballyhoo Cosmopolitan's productions and Davies' films in particular. Fulsome reviews, full-page rotogravures, and extensive coverage of premieres were spread before audiences that were increasingly eager to know about the on- and off-screen activities of their favorite stars. Hearst's foray into serials had taught him the value of marketing, including issuing new editions of the novels that Davies had filmed. A full-color dust jacket featured Davies in her movie role, while the title page announced the publication to be a "Marion Davies Edition."

The relentless publicity became the subject of mirth inside the film industry, capped by actress Beatrice Lillie's remark when first shown the lights of Los Angeles. "How wonderful!" said Lillie. "I suppose later they all merge and spell 'Marion Davies!' "[23]

Davies' box office results varied widely. One cinema historian speculated:

> She was a victim of her relationship with Hearst—a small portion of the public was offended by the unorthodox nature of the liaison—and she

Top: To promote Davies' movies, novels were often reissued with full-color dust jackets featuring the actress, with title pages proclaiming a "Marion Davies Edition." Above: In 1933, Davies' starring role in Peg o' My Heart *was advertised widely, even in the* Popsicle Movie Star Medallions *series.*

NEW THEATRE

DRAMA FILM DANCE

AUGUST 1935 15¢

IELLA PARSONS—HEARST'S HOLLYWOOD STOOGE by JOEL FAITH

HIBALD MacLEISH • HAROLD CLURMAN • ILYA EHRENBURG

Top: Hearst columnist Louella Parsons drew the attention of the August 1935 issue of New Theatre, *a publication of the New Theatre League.*
Above: Davies was featured on a number of fan magazine covers throughout her career, including this 1929 edition of Photoplay.

was also a victim of publicity overkill. Rarely a day went by without the Hearst papers mentioning her, usually with superlatives, and Davies served up daily with breakfast toast and coffee was too rich a diet for the average citizen. But the biggest problem was her early Cosmopolitan vehicles. For the most part, they were either stilted historical pageants or soupy romances, so overproduced that Davies was nearly suffocated by the elaborate pictorial values. And it didn't help that she was being forced to ape Mary Pickford, whom she resembled in face, but not in figure or spirit.[24]

Knighthood was also notable for the addition of movie columnist Louella Parsons to the roster of Hearst writers. Parsons, who was covering stage and screen events for the New York *Telegraph*, came to Hearst's attention when she lauded the Davies performance. She recalled,

It was popular in those days to "get out the hatchet" to earn our salaries—and so, when I couldn't honestly find anything to pick on Marion about, I wrote an editorial blasting William Randolph Hearst for bragging about spending so much money on the picture. Addressing my remarks personally to Mr. Hearst I wrote: "Why don't you give Marion Davies a chance? She is a good actress, a beauty and

a comedy-starring bet. Why talk about how much was spent on the lovely costumes and the production costs?"[25]

Hearst—good-natured about his public roasting at the hands of a rival paper's reporter—offered Parsons a job, increasing her salary from $110 to $250 per week. Parsons submitted an elaborate contract that "called for everything under the sun—all in my favor." Hearst refused to sign anything but a standard agreement. Eventually he capitulated, requesting Parsons' presence along with the contested contract. "Mr. Hearst looked at it a minute—then picked up the dilapidated piece of paper. Suddenly, he glanced up, smiling. 'I'm disappointed in you,' he said. 'Why?' I quaked. 'Miss Parsons,' he said, 'you forgot to ask for hairpins.' "[26]

Thus began the powerful career of the motion picture industry's foremost gossip columnist, whose zeal for the inside scoop in the film colony often outstripped her accuracy as well as her syntax. Calling herself the "Gay Illiterate," Parsons conceded "details" were often lost in the rush toward timely publication.

Hearst had greater difficulty finding producers to work for Cosmopolitan who shared his attention to detail. Just as he would analyze an ailing newspaper, Hearst summed up the problems of a 1923 Cosmopolitan production, *Under the Red Robe,*

80

starring Alma Rubens:

> It is an outrage to spend seven hundred thousand dollars on a picture and then neglect it the way this picture has been neglected—because that is what is the matter with it. The scenario is very bad. It doesn't stick to the story. The direction is atrocious. The photography in most cases is miserably poor—ten years behind the times. Poor Alma Rubens hasn't anything to do and is terribly lighted....
>
> The dueling is childishly poor—only good when done by doubles—like the duel on horseback. The cutting is hopeless and the titles are jokes. We have got to start in now and recut the picture entirely from the beginning. Then we have got to retake a lot of stuff and add more expense. Finally, I hope we will have a reasonably good picture—the kind that should have been made for three hundred thousand dollars.
>
> I have got to make some drastic changes and the first thing is to get some folks who will attend to business.[27]

In 1924, Hearst joined the general exodus to California, moving Cosmopolitan Productions from its studio in New York's Harlem to Hollywood, where he made new alliances. At the conclusion of Paramount's contract to distribute Hearst's films, pioneer movie producer Samuel Goldwyn won the rights to release Cosmopolitan films, beginning with the 1923 Davies costume epic, *Little Old New York*. The other stars under contract to Cosmopolitan, including Alma Rubens and Lionel Barrymore, also came west.

One of Hearst's great strategic decisions, the contract was even more valuable when Goldwyn's company merged within the year to form Metro-Goldwyn-Mayer, which soon became the most powerful studio in Hollywood. Ironically, Goldwyn was forced out before the MGM deal was struck, never working for the prestigious company that bore his name.

Cosmopolitan's feature films were distributed to the chain of theaters controlled by Loew's, Inc., MGM's parent company. According to the agreement, MGM bore the cost of producing all Cosmopolitan films and paid Davies $10,000 per week, a stratospheric sum matched only by the salaries of the most popular stars.

In return, Hearst agreed to split the profits of the Davies productions equally with MGM and to produce the Hearst Metrotone News, whose profits would also be divided in half. As perhaps the most important facet of the contract, Hearst agreed not only to publicize all MGM productions, but also to decide solely which films would receive the Cosmopolitan Productions imprimatur, guaranteeing even greater exposure in Hearst publications.[28]

Hearst proved to be a shrewd judge of box office potential. Two of his initial selections were *The Torrent* and

The 1933 Davies film Going Hollywood *helped launch Bing Crosby's movie career.* Marianne, *Davies' first talkie, was released in 1929.*

Cosmopolitan Productions releases such as Our Dancing Daughters *(1928) with Joan Crawford and* The Torrent *(1926) with Greta Garbo helped popularize Art Deco fashions and décor.*

The Temptress, the first American films of a import named Greta Garbo. MGM sought the services of noted Finnish-born director Mauritz Stiller and accepted his terms, which included a contract for his Swedish protégée. Ironically, Stiller's career did not blossom in America, and he soon returned to Sweden. Garbo remained, her career launched with the immeasurable assistance of the Hearst press.

The 1928 landmark film *Our Dancing Daughters* was released as a Cosmopolitan production. One of the first films to speak for a generation, *Daughters* told the story of the quintessential '20s flapper, popularized Art Deco decor, and propelled Joan Crawford from a contract player to the ranks of stardom.

The 1933 Cosmopolitan production *Gabriel Over the White House* provided Hearst with the means to express his political sentiments outside

the editorial pages. Both the screen-writer, Carey Wilson, and the producer, Walter Wanger, recall Hearst actively participating on this film, even to the point of writing or rewriting the presidential speeches used in the movie.

President Jud Hammond (played by Walter Huston) responds passively to the economic blight of the Depression, satisfying only the corrupt political machine that secured his election. Through the intervention of a reporter (assisted by the Angel Gabriel), Hammond abandons his ineffectual Hoover-like policies and transforms himself into "a dictatorial presence made in differing parts of Theodore Roosevelt, Abraham Lincoln, and Huey Long. [Hammond] is granite in feature, solemn in word, aggressive in manner, and unconstitutional in action."[29]

Hammond dismisses both Congress and his Cabinet and declares martial law in the name of expediency. The president creates a government-funded "Army of Construction" to employ the jobless, which in turn primes the nation's economy. Hammond eliminates gangsters, the well-publicized "public enemy" of the period, by repealing Prohibition and ordering the execution of the major mobster who resists his crackdown. Then, with a simplicity found only in the movies, "[Hammond's] earthly work is complete and there is no longer any need for a dictator. To reassure the audience that things will revert to the pre-Depression age, the film has Jud expire quite conveniently. He signs an international peace pact...with Lincoln's quill...lapses into a coma [and] dies a martyr for his country."[30]

Powerful columnist Walter Lippmann hated the film, writing,

> As a sample of what the movies can do for the political education of mankind, Gabriel is not so promising.... Gabriel is the infantile world of irresistible wishes. More specifically, it is a dramatization of Mr. Hearst's editorials.[31]

Hearst had not endorsed Roosevelt's presidential aspirations until it became clear that Hearst's first choice, John Nance Garner of Texas, could not swing the necessary votes on the convention floor. Hearst agreed at the eleventh hour to release California's crucial delegates to Roosevelt, in return for Garner's nomination as vice-president.

Although he would soon break with Roosevelt, primarily over the issue of taxes on wealth, Hearst agreed with FDR that the first hundred days of the Roosevelt administration were crucial. *Gabriel Over the White House*, containing several references to the recent 1932 Presidential campaign, was a direct effort on Hearst's part to smooth the path for the real-life president he had helped into office.[32]

The greatest critical and financial success of the Cosmopolitan/MGM collaboration was the 1934 production of *Manhattan Melodrama*, an aptly titled film featuring the first teaming of Myrna Loy and William Powell, who were joined by box office king Clark Gable. Long lines formed to see this picture, which gained additional publicity when FBI agents gunned down gangster John Dillinger as he emerged from a screening at Chicago's Biograph Theater.

During the years of the Cosmopolitan/MGM partnership, Marion Davies gave her finest performances. Still turning out the costume dramas Hearst favored, Davies also found time to star in several comedies. The most successful of these, and widely regarded as her finest films, are *The Patsy* and *Show People*, both made in 1928 and both directed by King Vidor, who had

Myrna Loy and Clark Gable starred in Manhattan Melodrama *(1934), one of Cosmopolitan's most successful productions.*

Sheet music from the Cosmopolitan film Hearts Divided *(1936), starring Marion Davies with singer Dick Powell.*

achieved great success with his epic films, *The Crowd* and *The Big Parade*.

Davies' skill as a light comedienne and gift for mimicry, freed from the burdens of epic historical events and ponderous dialogue, are fully evident in the Vidor comedies. *The Patsy*, a variation on the Cinderella theme, finds Davies slighted by her mother (Marie Dressler), who consistently favors Davies' glamorous and popular sister. In the course of the plot, Davies renders deft and devastating impressions of silent stars Lillian Gish, Pola Negri, and Mae Murray. The fan magazine *Photoplay* was entranced, stating,

> After two or three reels of this one the director tossed away his script—maybe his megaphone, too—and turned the picture over to Marion Davies. Which was a very smart thing to do, for when Marion cuts loose with clowning the result is that sort of comedy which reflects its results in crowded theaters.[33]

Cosmopolitan and MGM parted company in 1935, largely because Hearst believed that the choice roles (in particular, Marie Antoinette and Elizabeth Barrett Browning) were going to Norma Shearer, who was married to powerful producer Irving Thalberg. The only remedy, Hearst believed, was moving Cosmopolitan to Warner Brothers. MGM head Louis B. Mayer, who valued Hearst's friendship as much as his influence, attempted to

dissuade him, but failed. The well-publicized Davies dressing room (actually a fourteen-room house) was cut into sections and hauled on several flatbed trucks across the Hollywood hills to her new studio.

Eager to please, Warner's executives at once suggested that Davies play Arabella Bishop in *Captain Blood* opposite Errol Flynn. There is no record of Hearst's response, but Olivia de Havilland went on to play the role. Davies made only four pictures at her new studio; none was considered a great critical or financial success.

By the spring of 1937, Hearst was upset about the lack of starring roles suitable for Davies. Ella ("Bill") Williams, the Cosmopolitan liaison at the studio, wrote to Jack Warner about the situation, warning,

> [Hearst] said one thing that Metro did was to get stories for Marion, realizing that she was a star and the stories were about and for her…. He said that he has been very unhappy on this last picture [*Ever Since Eve* with Robert Montgomery], fighting for everything he has gotten and…having Marion look like a stick…. He said, "Maybe this is what [the Warner brothers] want here. Maybe they would prefer getting out of our contract."[34]

Davies decided to retire, but Hearst moved his production company to Twentieth Century-Fox, an association that lasted two years and co-produced *Young Mr. Lincoln* with Henry Fonda.

Hearst's influence as a film producer, coupled with his media power, made him an important member of Hollywood society. San Simeon, although located over two hundred miles north of the studios, beckoned to those in the film colony eager to advance their careers. Those who received the coveted invitations were drawn from a wide circle of friends, family, Hearst executives, politicians, journalists, celebrities, athletes, as well as the predictable directors, producers, and stars. Actors playing opposite Marion Davies were often invited to the hilltop to rehearse for an extended period of time.

The only recourse for those not invited to the estate was to read about it in the popular press. In 1931, *Fortune* magazine described a San Simeon visit for its readers, beginning with the arrival of Hearst's private railcar at the San Luis Obispo train station:

> Pilgrims of the private train, arising leisurely, are motored… forty-three miles and, at San Simeon, turn inland and ascend to the castle above in the hills… The road up [is] a beautiful, wide, carefully laid gravel road whose windings flatten a slope so steep that [as a child] Hearst clung to the tail of a horse to be pulled up…At the base of this hill you passed the airfield on which may land late Hearst newspapers from [distant] cities…. Continue on

up the road, through what will be Sequoia forests a thousand-odd years from now, then give it one last swing and end it…. Standing there, you can look back, out over the hills to the Pacific; then look around you to find Moorish palaces amid enchanted gardens… set off by the great twin towers of the Spanish mission cathedral which is Casa Grande. You are now in the heart of the Hearst estate.[35]

Adela Rogers St. Johns, a respected screenwriter and author, made her first trip to San Simeon with Hearst himself. Planning to travel to San Simeon to see one of the Hearst magazine executives, St. Johns received a call in Los Angeles from Hearst's secretary, Joseph Willicombe.

> "The Chief is driving up this evening and he says you may come with him if you care to." I said I cared to…. To most of us who worked for Mr. Hearst he came above all earthly authority and just below Jove…on Mount Olympus, and I was going to ride from Hollywood to San Simeon, two hundred and fifty miles, alone in an automobile with him….

St. Johns overcame her awe and soon she was engaged in lively conversation with her boss about writing, college experiences, and life in California.

> We went into a roadside diner at Los Alamos and sat on stools and Mr. Hearst said he recommended the ham and eggs or the chili so I had both. Then we got back on the

Silent film stars Gloria Swanson, Charlie Chaplin, and Marion Davies pose at a party at the Ambassador Hotel in Los Angeles.

Hearst's weekend guests at a 1926 party for United Artists included John Gilbert, reclining in front, with Buster Keaton and Constance Talmadge behind him and Greta Garbo, center, looking down. Norma Shearer and Irving Thalberg, dressed for tennis, face the camera at far right.

road. Coming out of San Luis Obispo, where we took Coast Highway 1 by Morro Bay…we ran into…fog,…which thickened so the car had to cut through it like a knife. We were on a one-lane…dirt road with no lights, no white lines, our car lights were dim. The sea was on one side, a cliff high on the other, the car twisted…. Our driver hung his head out [the window]… Then Mr. Hearst gently said, "Here's a shoulder, pull off and I will drive." …Here we have a trained chauffeur, it's his business, I said to myself. Mr. William Randolph Hearst owns gold mines and runs 999 newspapers and can tell presidents what to do so he thinks he can drive….

Fifty miles to San Simeon. Though from time to time I heard a car or the rocks bouncing down from the cliff edge, I never saw anything. Our way was as wide as

the car's wheels, no wider, and as spiral as a corkscrew. We drove at a steady, fast pace, once or twice we stopped to let a gate swing open under the invisible guidance of a Mexican cowboy, we curved, climbed without a single hesitation or inch of deviation, and came to a perfect stop on the circular drive in front of what we then called the Three Cottages.

On the terrace of one of the white-stucco three-story "cottages" that were the only houses then finished, Mr. Hearst bowed and told me a courteous good night and thanked me for my company.[36]

Actor and assistant director Harry Crocker recalled his many visits to San Simeon in his memoirs, including this after-dinner entertainment:

Raquel Miller, the Spanish singer was under discussion. [Chaplin] seized a scarf, threw it across his shoulders and amused Eleanor Glyn, Ethel Barrymore, Beatrice Lillie, Mr. and Mrs. [Holbrook] Blinn, Eleanor Boardman, King Vidor, and many others in a perfect imitation of the gestures of the famous Raquel, singing her Spanish songs in a marvelous jargon which was an exact mimicry of the sound of the Spanish language. "And all the Spanish he knows," remarked Irvin Cobb, "is the names of three cigars."[37]

Actor Joel McCrea, a guest in the 1930s, recalled one noteworthy birthday party where Hearst was toasted with champagne by the head of every major movie studio in Hollywood. At another gathering, McCrea conversed with an older woman who was dressed very simply. He then discovered her name was Julia Morgan and that his mother had attended Berkeley with her. Still exchanging stories, Morgan and McCrea left the Refectory.

> I put my arm around her and was talking about my mother… Mr. Hearst saw that, so he came up to me afterward. Usually he was aloof of most things… but he came up and said, "How did you happen to know Miss Morgan? She's my architect. She takes castles down in Spain and puts them on a boat and sends them back." And I said, "Well, she [and] my mother graduated [together] and they were Kappa Alpha Beta and room-mates…"[38]

From that moment, Hearst took special interest in McCrea's career, even interceding on his behalf without McCrea's knowledge to studio chief Louis B. Mayer.

Adela Rogers St. Johns remembered,

> There was a motion picture run every single night come hell or high water…and to this every guest whether exalted or unimportant had to go. And stay. This was, I think, partly because Mr. Hearst loved movies and partly because he had a sort of paternal care for his high-spirited and temperamental

Hearst celebrated his 75th birthday with a costume party at Marion Davies' Santa Monica beach house, where he posed with (from left) Jack L. Warner, Raoul Walsh, Davies, and an unidentified guest.

guests and thought it might be dangerous for them to wander about at night, alone or in couples. (It often was.)[39]

St. Johns believed the origin of the popular misconception that death could not be mentioned in Hearst's presence derived from the popular song, "(I'll Be Glad When You're Dead) You Rascal, You." One evening after the movie screening, some of the younger guests played the record "over and over. At a point of nausea, Mr. Hearst removed it, broke it in two, and put the pieces in the fireplace saying, 'I feel we have heard that often enough. I find it a vulgar lyric and a vapid tune. Let us have something gay.' "[40]

Those who incurred Hearst's displeasure often suffered more than a broken record. Walter Wanger, who would work with Hearst on Cosmopolitan films, recalls an unintentional

Hearst on the steps of St. Donat's, his castle in Wales, which he purchased in 1925.

slight that led to his temporary banishment.

We were great friends, but I had a feud with him once because of a picture called *Washington Merry-Go-Round*. In the first scene, Rosalind Russell played a Washington hostess sitting at the head of a table surrounded by national figures. One was a newspaper owner trying to involve us in a war. On account of my great friendship with Hearst, I had purposely picked a little fellow with a black mustache for the role. It was Ralph Morgan, brother of Frank Morgan. At the last minute, [Morgan backed out and the casting director] hired an actor who was a bit man and came to the screen just like William Randolph Hearst. I didn't want to do retakes because of a tight budget, and it was one of my first independent pictures. We decided to let it go, but I was terrified. The picture came out and everybody ran to Hearst. "See what your friend Walter Wanger has done."

I was banned from the Hearst papers. They wouldn't even take our advertising. "Why don't you apologize?" Louella asked me. I refused and just let it ride. Six months to a year later, Marion called up. "Why don't you come to see us anymore?" "Well, I heard W.R. was angry with me," I

answered. She turned around and inquired, "W.R., Walter says he thought you were angry with him. Isn't that the silliest thing?" The ban had been lifted. He was like a big child, and yet he was an amazing man in many ways.[41]

Hearst friend and advisor John Francis Neylan once noted,

Money as such bores him…. He is a builder. He wants to build buildings, newspapers, magazines, hotels, ranches. His idea is to build, build, build all the time…. In his makeup there is just a blank space in relation to money.[42]

Hearst's "blank space" was soon filled with the advice of lawyers and financial consultants. By early 1937, Hearst's unrestrained buying sprees were catching up to him and the condition of his personal and business finances was precarious. The advent of Roosevelt's New Deal and a sharp rise in taxes on personal wealth and large corporations also contributed to his financial woes. It was estimated that there were at least ninety companies under the Hearst Corporation name; each had borrowed from banks and other Hearst companies until the indebtedness was estimated at $126 million.[43]

In June, Hearst signed over his controlling stock in the primary holding corporation to Judge Clarence J. Shearn. Hearst retained control of editorial policy, but his finances were now in other hands for the first time since he inherited his patrimony in 1919.

The retrenchment of the Hearst Corporation was in capable hands. Shearn directed the sale of the six Hearst papers that operated at a deficit, along with seven of the ten Hearst radio stations. Only one Hearst magazine, *Pictorial Review*, ceased publication; Hearst's two wire services were merged into one company. In the first year Shearn managed to save the Hearst Corporation $5 million.

It was less easy to persuade Hearst to part with his vast treasure trove of antiquities or his magnificent estates. The advisors recommended that at least two-thirds of the art must be sold to avoid inheritance taxes and to provide a cash infusion to the corporation. Appraisers determined that Hearst had collected 504 separate categories of art, twenty of which were outstanding in quality. Hearst's accumulation of English silver, English furniture, armor, tapestries, and Hispano-Moresque pottery were ranked among the finest private collections in the world.

The fifth floor of Gimbel Brothers department store was transformed, according to the *Saturday Evening Post*, into a "gigantic bazaar of the arts." Ten thousand art objects, including paneling, ceilings, stained glass, paintings, and sculpture, covered 100,000 square feet of space in the store. The initial

Winston Churchill, recently turned out of office in Britain, visited California in 1929. In addition to a stay at San Simeon, Churchill visited MGM's back lot with Hearst and studio head Louis B. Mayer (right).

two-month period, during which Gimbel's assumed the role of agent and received a commission on each piece sold, was so successful it was extended for fourteen months. The *New York Times* noted, "Armor, of which Hearst had enough to stage a successful siege of his castle of St. Donat, sold from $4.50 up. Egyptian statuettes, tagged at 35, 60 and 95 cents, were among the fifteen thousand items...." The English silver, including pieces from the Tudor, Stuart, and early Georgian periods, were sold at Sotheby's London office.

Also sold during the period of retrenchment was Sacramenia, a twelfth-century Cistercian monastery Hearst had purchased outright in 1925. Hearst had originally commissioned art dealers Mildred and Arthur

Byne to locate and purchase a Gothic cloister, but the Bynes discovered the entire monastery was available. All of the structures were dismantled stone by stone (with the exception of the kitchen and the lay brothers' refectory) and shipped to New York in numbered crates.

The straw that was used as packing material was banned by the U.S. Agricultural Department, forcing the stones to be uncrated and repacked before they left Spain. The cost of the shipping alone was estimated at $400,000. Hearst's plans to reconstruct the monastery were abandoned after his financial difficulties in the late 1930s. Eventually the stones were sold for $19,000 and shipped to North Miami Beach, Florida, where the building was reconstructed as an Episcopalian church.[44]

Hearst's financial pressures also curtailed building at San Simeon. He

had followed George Hearst's practice of buying up parcels of land from neighbors, until his holdings at San Simeon approached 260,000 acres. Hedda Hopper, Parsons' rival gossip columnist, reminisced in her column about one of her last visits to the estate.

> One day when I was standing on the balcony outside the library showing Lady Irene Ravensdale how much land W.R. owned, I swept my arm in a circle and said, "He owns all of these 375,000 [sic] acres except that mountain away off there in the distance." Then a thin voice came over my shoulder, "Hedda, I own that, too."[45]

Above: Hearst poses in 1937 with gossip columnist Hedda Hopper at a circus-themed costume party at Davies' beach house in Santa Monica.
Right: In 1935, Hearst reacted to California's new state income tax by threatening to sell his San Simeon estate.

During World War II, Hearst retreated with Davies to Wyntoon because it was generally believed that San Simeon was vulnerable to Japanese attack. After the war he returned to San Simeon, but in 1947 a heart attack forced him to leave the estate for the last time. He retreated to a relatively modest Beverly Hills estate at 1007 Lexington Drive to be close to the specialists who attempted to maintain his faltering health.

On August 14, 1951, William Randolph Hearst died at the age of 88 from "several cerebral vascular accidents" together with the effects of "ailments of advanced age." His widow and five sons gathered in San Francisco for the funeral in San Francisco and the interment at Cypress Lawn Cemetery in Colma, California. His will, at 125 pages, was the longest ever filed in California. A portion of the estate, believed to total nearly $220 million, was left in trust to his family; the remainder was bequeathed to the California Charities (now the Hearst Foundation) as a charitable trust.[46]

Headlines in newspapers around the world marked his passing. *Life* magazine, in a ten-page obituary, eulogized Hearst as "…more than a man; he was the inventor, purveyor, prolificator and practitioner of a phenomenon known as Hearst Journalism…. In part it was a one-man fireworks display."[47]

But for all his wealth and influence, Hearst remains an enigmatic figure, little known and even less understood, a man whose public character and private inclinations often seemed diametrically opposed. His energies and enthusiasms outstripped every competitor; his name still inspires debate. Perhaps the only person who was not mystified was Hearst himself. Shortly before his death, he was quoted as saying, "If I had my life to live over again, I would be a newspaper man, and merely try to be a better one."[48]

W. R. Hearst relaxes at Wyntoon in 1935 with his beloved dachshund, Gandhi.

End Notes

Chapter One

1. William Hearst, letter to George Hearst, Autumn 1884, William Randolph Hearst Papers, Bancroft Library, U of California, Berkeley. Hereafter cited as WRH Papers.

2. WRH Papers, Autumn 1884.

3. *Franklin County Tribune* [Union, Missouri] Nov. 24, 1899 (qtd. in Ralph Gregory, "George Hearst in Missouri," *Missouri Historical Society Bulletin* 21 [1965] 77).

4. Cora Older, *George Hearst, Pioneer* (Los Angeles: Westernlore, 1966) 84.

5. George Hearst, letter to Joseph Funk, Mar. 18, 1858, read into transcript of Case 120, 1876, United States Circuit Ct., Eastern Missouri District (Sept. Term, 1876) 157–8 (qtd. in Gregory 62).

6. Gregory 62.

7. Older 113.

8. Crawford County [Missouri] Marriage Contracts, Book A, Nos. 1, 4, 5.

9. Older 120.

10. W.A. Swanberg, *Citizen Hearst* (New York: Scribners, 1961) 7.

11. *Sacramento Bee*, 1865 (qtd. in John Bruce, *Gaudy Century* [New York: Random, 1948] 200).

12. James Ben Ali Haggin (1821–1914) was born into a prominent Kentucky family. (His middle name comes from his maternal grandfather, who was a Turkish physician.) Haggin went to Sacramento in 1850 where he practiced law with Milton S. Latham. Haggin and his brother-in-law, Lloyd Tevis, moved their land and brokerage business to San Francisco in 1853 and eventually began a long association with George Hearst.

13. Phoebe Hearst, letter to George Hearst, Mar. 25, 1873, Phoebe Apperson Hearst Papers, Bancroft Library, U of California, Berkeley. Hereafter cited as PAH Papers.

14. Swanberg, *Citizen Hearst* 14.

15. PAH Papers, June 15, 1873.

16. PAH Papers, Dec. 15, 1873.

17. PAH Papers, June 30, 1873.

18. PAH Papers, Oct. 5, 1873.

19. PAH Papers, Dec. 3, 1873.

20. PAH Papers, Dec. 3, 1873.

21. PAH Papers, Dec. 3, 1873.

22. Bill Harlan, "American Dream Fades for Long-time Mine: Homestake Mine Was Last El Dorado of the West." *Rapid City Journal*, n.d. http://www.deadwood discovered.com/history/homestake.html

23. George Hearst, letter to James Haggin, n.d. (qtd. in Michael Cieply, "The Loded Hearst," *Westways* 73 [1981] 76-77).

24. Lloyd Tevis (1824–1899) moved to California in 1849 from his native Kentucky. After an unsuccessful stint as a prospector, he opened a land office in Sacramento with his brother-in-law, James Haggin. He moved to San Francisco in 1853 to practice law with the firm of Crockett, Page and Tevis, but partnership with J.B. Haggin soon became his primary business.

25. Cieply 34.

26. George Hearst, letter to James Haggin, Mar. 1879 (qtd. in Cieply 35).

27. George Hearst, letter to James Haggin, n.d. (qtd. in Cieply 78).

28. "Homestake Mining Company," *Hoover's Online*, Nov. 27, 2004. http://premium. hoovers.com/subscribe/co/boneyard/factsheet.xhtml?ID=10739

29. Richard White, *Your Misfortune and None of My Own: A New History of the American West* (Norman: U of Oklahoma P, 1991) 266.

30. William Randolph Hearst, letter to George Hearst, Mar. 29, 1878, George Hearst Papers, Bancroft Library, U of California, Berkeley. Hereafter cited as GH Papers.

31. GH Papers, Feb. 5, 1879.

32. All Thomas Barry passages from typescript of diary for June 6, 7, 11 and Aug. 24, 1879, Thomas Barry Diary, Bancroft Library, U of California, Berkeley.

33. PAH Papers, [c. Autumn, 1879].

34. PAH Papers, Dec. 30, 1882.

35. WRH Papers, Autumn 1884.

36. WRH Papers, [1884].

37. WRH Papers, 1885.

38. WRH Papers, [Apr. 29, 1884].

39. WRH Papers, letters, n.d. [believed to be 1884].

40. PAH Papers, Oct. 4, 1885.

41. *Collier's* Sept. 22, 1906.

42. WRH Papers, Spring 1885. As *Time* later noted, "… As managing editor of the *Lampoon*, Mr. Hearst first sniffed…the drug of printer's ink." Aug. 15, 1927: 21.

43. WRH Papers, Nov. 23, 1885.

44. WRH Papers, [1885].

45. WRH Papers, Nov. 23, 1885.

46. Swanberg, *Citizen Hearst* 37.

47. *San Francisco Examiner*, Mar. 4, 1887, 2.

Chapter Two

1. Edwin Emery, *The Press in America* (Englewood Cliffs, N.J.: Prentice-Hall, 1962) 346.

2. Garth Jowett, *Film: The Democratic Art* (Boston: Little, Brown and Company, 1976) 16-17.

3. *San Francisco Examiner*, Apr. 3, 1887.

4. Warren Hinckle, " 'Leaping Higher, Higher' Hearst Re-invented the Wheel of Journalism," *The Examiner Centennial* [San Francisco], Mar. 1, 1987, special edition: 2.

5. WRH Papers, [1887].

6. Swanberg, *Citizen Hearst* 53.

7. Will Irwin, "The Fourth Current," *Collier's* Feb. 18, 1911: 14, and John Tebbel, *The Life and Good Times of William Randolph Hearst* (New York: E.P. Dutton, 1952) 99-100.

8. WRH Papers, [1887].

9. Swanberg, *Citizen Hearst* 43.

10. Oscar Lewis, *The Big Four* (New York: Knopf, 1946) 349.

11. Patricia Schofler, "A Glorious Adventure…" *American History Illustrated* 15.10 (1981): 31.

12. Oscar Lewis, *Bay Window Bohemia* (Garden City, New York: Doubleday, 1956): 138-139.

13. Coblentz 48.

14. WRH Papers, [1887].

15. PAH Papers, Aug. 7, 1888.

16. Coblentz 34-35.

17. *New York Times*, Mar. 1, 1891.

18. PAH Papers, [1894].

19. W.A. Swanberg, *Pulitzer* (New York: Scribner's, 1967) 206.

20. Tebbel 126.

[21] Swanberg, *Pulitzer* 205.

[22] Tebbel 116-117.

[23] Swanberg, *Citizen Hearst* 83.

[24] Irwin 18.

[25] Irwin 18.

[26] Sarah D. Lowrie, "Comic Strips," *The Forum* 79.4 (1928) 527.

[27] Lowrie 528.

[28] Lowrie 530.

[29] *New York Journal* Feb. 22, 1906.

[30] *New York Journal* Nov. 8, 1896.

[31] *New York Journal* Oct. 21, 1900.

[32] Swanberg, *Pulitzer* 224.

[33] Swanberg, *Pulitzer* 226.

[34] Swanberg, *Pulitzer* 226.

[35] Marcus Wilkerson, *Public Opinion and the Spanish-American War: A Study in War Propaganda* (1932; New York: Russell & Russell, 1967) 33.

[36] Swanberg, *Citizen Hearst* 149.

[37] PAH Papers, [1898].

[38] *New York Times*, July 1, 1898.

[39] Emery 374.

[40] Soon Jin Kim, "An Anatomy of the Hearst Press Campaign to Fortify an American Isthmian Canal," diss., U of Maryland, 1982, 87.

[41] George Murray, *The Madhouse on Madison Street* (Chicago: Follett, 1965) ix.

[42] *New York Times*, Oct. 28, 1900.

Chapter Three

[1] Adela Rogers St. Johns, *The Honeycomb* (Garden City: Doubleday, 1969) 131-2.

[2] David Nasaw, *The Chief: The Life of William Randolph Hearst* (Boston: Houghton Mifflin, 2000) 115.

[3] Upton Sinclair, *The Industrial Republic* (New York: Doubleday, Page, 1907) 203.

[4] Swanberg, *Citizen Hearst* 219.

[5] Elbert later changed his name to David Whitmire.

[6] Coblentz 68-69.

[7] Millicent Hearst, letter to Phoebe Apperson Hearst, [Spring 1906], Hearst Family Papers, Bancroft Library, U of California, Berkeley. Hereafter cited as HF Papers.

[8] New York American, n.d. (qtd. in Gordon Thomas and Max Morgan Witts, *The San Francisco Earthquake* [New York: Stein and Day, 1971] 83).

[9] John K. Winkler, *William Randolph Hearst: A New Appraisal* (New York: Hastings, 1955) 183.

[10] Winkler 183.

[11] HF Papers, July 30, 1906.

[12] Hearst was representing this same district in Congress when he submitted a bill requesting federal funds disaster relief and the construction of new government buildings in the wake of the San Francisco earthquake and fire.

[13] *New York Times* Dec. 10, 1905 (qtd. in David Sarasohn, "Power Without Glory: Hearst in the Progressive Era," *Journalism Quarterly* 53.3 [1976]: 476-477).

[14] Sarasohn 477.

[15] Swanberg, *Citizen Hearst* 236.

[16] *New York Evening Post* Mar, 1, 1904: 16.

[17] Sarasohn 474.

[18] *New York World* 7 Nov. 1906. Historian Arthur Schlesinger, Jr. wrote that Hearst's political beliefs "follow a long trajectory from left to right," but recent revisionist thinking postulates that Hearst's political views actually changed very little from the turn of the century until his death fifty years later. This static ideology left Hearst with turn-of-the-century causes that were unable to keep pace with more progressive New Deal philosophies. Arthur Schlesinger, Jr., *The Age of Roosevelt*, vol. 3 (Boston: Houghton-Mifflin, 1960) 84. See also Rodney P. Carlisle, "William Randolph Hearst: A Fascist Reputation Reconsidered," *Journalism Quarterly* 50.1 (1973): 125-133.

[19] HF Papers, Oct. 29, 1907.

[20] David S. Hulfish (qtd. in Raymond Fielding, *The American Newsreel: 1911-1967* [Norman: U of Oklahoma P, 1972] 64).

[21] *Moving Picture World* 7 Mar 1914 (qtd. in Fielding, 86).

[22] *Time* Nov. 23, 1936: 25.

[23] Fielding 188. The names of newsreels produced by these companies were Fox-Movietone News, Hearst Metrotone News, (later retitled News of the Day), Paramount News ("The Eyes and Ears of the World"), Pathé News and Universal News.

[24] Fielding 135.

[25] Terry Ramsaye, *A Million and One Nights: A Modern Classic* (1926; New York: Simon & Schuster, 1986) 310.

[26] Wallace E. Davies, "The Truth About Pearl White," *Films in Review* Nov. 1959: 541.

[27] Kalton Lahue, *Continued Next Week: A History of the Moving Picture Serial* (Norman: U of Oklahoma P, 1964) 8. The fact that Pauline continues to "pull people" today is a bit paradoxical, for its production values are crude. Made only two years after the concept of serialization had been applied to motion pictures, *The Perils of Pauline* was quickly outstripped by its immediate successors, with varying camera angles, more plot twists and more realistic action.

[28] Lahue 12.

[29] Ramsaye 662.

[30] Raymond William Stedman, *The Serials: Suspense and Drama by Installment* (Norman: U of Oklahoma P, 1971) 16.

[31] Ishbel Ross, *Ladies of the Press* (1936; New York: Arno P, 1974). 79. Another 1916 Hearst-Pathé venture, *The Mysteries of Myra*, began the trend toward passive heroines. Myra was dependent upon the actions of others for her salvation, primarily her quick-thinking fiancé, who always intervened in the nick of time.

[32] Irene Castle, *Castles in the Air* (1958; New York: Da Capo P, 1980): 145.

[33] Winkler 227.

[34] Fred Lawrence Guiles, *Marion Davies* (New York: McGraw-Hill, 1972) 120.

[35] Guiles 43-44.

[36] Marion Davies, *The Times We Had: Life with William Randolph Hearst* (Indianapolis: Bobbs-Merrill, 1975) 9, 10.

[37] *New York American* May 6, 1918.

[38] *New York Times* (qtd. in Guiles 376).

[39] Delight Evans, "Galatea on Riverside Drive," *Photoplay* Oct. 1919: 36.

[40] *San Francisco Examiner*, Apr. 14, 1919.

[41] Nasaw 279. http://www.westegg.com/inflation/

Chapter Four

1 William Randolph Hearst, letter to Julia Morgan, Dec. 31, 1919, Julia Morgan Collection, Special Collections, California Polytechnic State U, San Luis Obispo. Hereafter cited as JM Collection.

2 Walter Steilberg, oral history interview with Sally Woodbridge, Julia Morgan Architectural History Project, ed. Suzanne B. Riess, vol. 1 (Berkeley: Regents of the U of Calif., 1976) 57.

3 William Randolph Hearst, Jr. with Jack Casserly, *The Hearsts: Father and Son* (Niwot, CO: Roberts Rinehart, 1991) 67.

4 Hearst retained Morgan in 1910 to design a residence in Sausalito, but the plans were abandoned when he moved to New York. In 1915, she completed a notable Mission Revival building for Hearst's *Los Angeles Examiner*.

5 Dec. 21, 1919, JM Collection.

6 Joseph Willicombe, letter to J.B. Lee, Mar. 23, 1921 and draft response from Julia Morgan to WRH, [1921], JM Collection.

7 Robert C. Pavlik, "The Design and Construction of La Cuesta Encantada, 1919–1948." Dept. of Parks and Recreation, San Simeon Region, ts., 1988, 14.

8 Sept. 13, 1919, JM Collection.

9 June 2, 1921, JM Collection.

10 May 19, 1924, JM Collection. See also correspondence between Morgan and Hearst for May and June of 1924, and May of 1928 for further discussion of this topic.

11 Feb. 19, 1927, JM Collection.

12 Feb. 7, 1927, JM Collection.

13 William Randolph Hearst, letter to C.C. Rossi, Feb. 16, 1927, JM Collection.

14 Apr. 1, 1927, JM Collection.

15 May 29, 1930; June 4, 1930, JM Collection.

16 Undated memo, PAH Papers.

17 Sara Holmes Boutelle, *Julia Morgan, Architect* (1988; New York: Abbeville, 1995) 219.

18 "Hearst Once Owned 2,000,000 Acres," *Editor & Publisher* Aug. 18, 1951: 10.

19 *Chicago Sun-Times*, Sept. 27, 1952. After Hearst's death, the financial settlements he made on his estranged wife were revealed when Millicent Hearst filed suit against his estate for payment of more than $2.5 million based on the two legal agreements: "Mrs. Hearst said the full payments under the two agreements never were made, although Mr. Hearst at times acknowledged the obligations and explained he was financially unable and would make them up later. When Mr. Hearst died he owed her approximately $216,500 under the 1921 agreement and $2.2 million under the 1927 agreement...."

20 Harry Bitner, "Hearst Was Last of Great Individualists," *Editor & Publisher* Aug. 18, 1951: 13.

21 "Hearst," *Fortune* Oct. 1935: 43.

22 Howard Mandelbaum and Eric Myers, *Screen Deco* (New York: St. Martin's, 1985) 7.

23 Charlie Chaplin, *My Autobiography* (New York: Simon, 1964) 331.

24 Gary Carey, *All the Stars in Heaven* (New York: Dutton, 1981) 114-15.

25 Louella Parsons, *The Gay Illiterate* (Garden City: Doubleday, 1944) 68.

26 Parsons 71-72.

27 Fred Lawrence Guiles, *Marion Davies* (New York: McGraw-Hill, 1972) 120-121.

28 Bernard Rosenberg and Harry Silverstein, *The Real Tinsel* (London: Macmillan, 1970) 114.

29 Andrew Bergman, *We're in the Money: Depression America and Its Films* (New York: Harper, 1972) 111.

30 Peter Roffman and Jim Purdy, *The Hollywood Social Problem Film: Madness, Despair, and Politics from the Depression to the Fifties* (Bloomington: Indiana UP, 1981) 69.

31 *Motion Picture Herald* Apr. 8, 1933: 1.

32 Rodney Carlisle, "William Randolph Hearst: A Fascist Reputation Reconsidered" *Journalism Quarterly* 50.1 (1973) 127-133.

33 *Photoplay* Apr. 22, 1928: 32.

34 Ella Williams, memo to J.L. Warner, qtd. in Rudy Behlmer, ed., *Inside Warner Bros. (1935-1951)* (New York: Viking, 1985) 38.

35 "Hearst at Home," *Fortune* May 1931: 57.

36 Adela Rogers St. Johns, *The Honeycomb* (Garden City: Doubleday, 1969) 124-128.

37 Harry Crocker, unpublished memoirs, "Small Talk About Big People," ts., 61-63, Harry Crocker Collection, Margaret Herrick Library, Academy of Motion Picture Arts and Sciences.

38 Joel McCrea, "Hearst, Hollywood and San Simeon: an Oral History Interview," ed. Nancy E. Loe. Dec. 5, 1982, Oral History Project, Hearst San Simeon State Historical Monument, 6–13.

39 St. Johns 140.

40 St. Johns 140.

41 Rosenberg 87.

42 Winkler 278.

43 Winkler 278.

44 Joanne E. Sowell, *The Monastery of Sacramenia and Twelfth-Century Cistercian Architecture in Spain*, diss., (Florida State U, 1985) 59-69. Sowell comments at length on the secrecy that surrounded the removal of a historical monument from Spain. Byne instructed both Morgan and Hearst never to mention the name of the monastery in their cables.

45 Hedda Hopper's Hollywood, ts., press release Aug. 29, 1957, Hedda Hopper Collection, Margaret Herrick Library, Academy of Motion Picture Arts and Sciences. The State Department of Parks and Recreation (formerly the State Division of Parks and Beaches) has managed the Monument since the transfer of ownership. On June 2, 1958, the Monument opened to the public for the first time.

46 Millicent Willson Hearst died in New York City in 1974 at the age of 92. Marion Davies died in California in 1961 at the age of 64.

47 *Life* Aug. 27, 1951: 22.

48 Winkler 1.

Bibliography

Secondary Sources

Behlmer, Rudy, ed., *Inside Warner Bros. (1935-1951)*. New York: Viking P, 1985.

Bergman, Andrew. *We're in the Money: Depression America and Its Films*. New York: Harper & Row, 1972.

Bitner, Harry M. "Hearst Was Last of Great Individualists." *Editor & Publisher* 18 Aug. 1951: 13.

Burgess, R.L. "Working for Hearst." *New Republic* 10 Aug. 1932: 340–342.

Carey, Gary. *All the Stars in Heaven*. New York: E.P. Dutton, 1981.

Carlisle, Rodney. "William Randolph Hearst: A Fascist Reputation Reconsidered." *Journalism Quarterly* 50.1 (1973): 125–133.

Castle, Irene. *Castles in the Air*. 1958. New York: DaCapo P, 1980.

Chaplin, Charles. *My Autobiography*. New York: Simon & Shuster, 1964.

Cieply, Michael. "The Loded Hearst." *Westways* 73.6 (1981): 32–35+.

Coblentz, Edmond D. *William Randolph Hearst: A Portrait in His Own Words*. New York: Simon & Schuster, 1952.

Editor & Publisher 18 Aug. 1951: 7+.

Evans, Delight. "Galatea on Riverside Drive." *Photoplay* Oct. 1919: 36.

Fielding, Raymond. *The American Newsreel: 1911–1967*. Norman: U of Oklahoma P, 1972.

Gregory, Ralph. "George Hearst in Missouri." *Missouri Historical Society Bulletin* 21.2 (1965): 75–86.

Guiles, Fred Lawrence. *Marion Davies*. New York: McGraw-Hill, 1972.

"Hearst." *Fortune* Oct. 1935: 42-55+.

"Hearst at Home." *Fortune* May 1931: 57+.

Irwin, Will. "The Fourth Current." *Collier's* 18 Feb. 1911: 14.

Lahue, Kalton C. *Continued Next Week: A History of the Moving Picture Serial*. Norman: U of Oklahoma P, 1964.

Lundberg, Ferdinand. *Imperial Hearst: A Social Biography*. New York: Equinox Cooperative P, 1936.

Mandelbaum, Howard and Eric Myers. *Screen Deco*. New York: St. Martin's P, 1985.

MacShane, Frank. "The Romantic World of William Randolph Hearst." *Centennial Review* 8.3 (1964): 292–305.

Milne, Tom. "Show People." *Sight and Sound* 37 (Fall 1968): 200–201.

Murray, George. *The Madhouse on Madison Street*. Chicago: Follett, 1965.

Nasaw, David. *The Chief: The Life of William Randolph Hearst*. New York: Houghton Mifflin, 2000.

Older, Cora. *George Hearst, Pioneer*. Los Angeles: Westernlore, 1966.

Parsons, Louella. *The Gay Illiterate*. Garden City: Doubleday, Doran and Co., 1944.

Peterson, Richard H. "Philanthropic Phoebe." *California History* 64.4 (1985): 284–289.

Roffman, Peter and Jim Purdy. *The Hollywood Social Problem Film: Madness, Despair, and Politics from the Depression to the Fifties*. Bloomington: Indiana UP, 1981.

Rosenberg, Bernard, and Harry Silverstein. *The Real Tinsel*. London: Macmillan, 1970.

Ross, Ishbel. *Ladies of the Press*. 1936. New York: Arno P, 1974.

St. Johns, Adela Rogers. *The Honeycomb*. Garden City: Doubleday, 1969.

Sarasohn, David. "Power Without Glory: Hearst in the Progressive Era." *Journalism Quarterly* 53.3 (1976): 474–482.

Sky, Alison and Michelle Stone. *Unbuilt America: Forgotten Architecture in the United States*. New York: McGraw-Hill, 1976.

Stedman, Raymond William. *The Serials: Suspense and Drama by Installment*. Norman: U of Oklahoma P, 1971.

Swanberg, W.A. *Citizen Hearst*. New York: Scribners, 1961.

—. *Pulitzer*. New York: Scribners, 1967.

Primary Sources

Academy of Motion Picture Arts and Sciences
   Harry Crocker Collection
   Hedda Hopper Collection

The Bancroft Library, University of California at Berkeley
   Thomas Barry Diary, 79/88z
   Hearst Family Papers, 85/3c (Cited as HF Papers)
   George Hearst Papers, 73/38 and 72/204c
   Phoebe Apperson Hearst Papers, 72/204c (Cited as PAH Papers)
   William Randolph Hearst Papers, 77/121 and 82/68c
     (Cited as WRH Papers)

California Polytechnic State University, San Luis Obispo
   Cora Older Collection on George Hearst
   Julia Morgan Collection (Cited as JM Collection)

Hearst San Simeon State Historical Monument
   Archives
   Oral History Collection